BLOOD AND BEAUTY

BLOOD AND BEAUTY

12 Combat Plays for Women

Terry Kroenung

iUniverse, Inc.
New York Lincoln Shanghai

BLOOD AND BEAUTY
12 Combat Plays for Women

iUniverse, Inc.

For information address:
iUniverse, Inc.
2021 Pine Lake Road, Suite 100
Lincoln, NE 68512
www.iuniverse.com

ISBN: 0-595-27920-1

Printed in the United States of America

To the Lady Cavaliers whose blood, beauty, brains, and blades spawned these plays.

Contents

DARK LADY

A play by Terry Kroenung
© 2002

SCENE: *Late 16th century London. The Poet's room; The Dark Lady's bedroom; Young Lord's house; the street.*

SET: *A rude desk and chair UR, with paper, quills, ink, etc. Ornately-appointed bed UL, with accompanying chair/table. Open area downstage. This is envisioned to be a thrust stage, but proscenium would work.*

NOTE: *There is no dialogue. The style should be somewhere between realism and dance, like a poem. ALL ACTION IS SET TO RAVEL'S "BOLERO". (The version I used was Leonard Bernstein and the New York Philharmonic, published in 1985. Others should be similar). Feel free to use other music, including original, as long as the end result is achieved.* **_Producers must resolve copyright issues on their own._**

EACH SECTION OF THE PLAY MATCHES UP WITH THE VARIOUS SECTIONS OF THE MUSIC. *The numbers I use correspond with the* <u>counter numbers</u> *on my CD player. I give them here as a guide only.*

(Lights come up UR on the Poet's area)

1

0.00—The **POET**, a balding, bearded, scruffy young man on the way up, not well-nourished or well-dressed, is writing at the desk. It is not a successful day. He agonizes over each word, scratches out, throws several sheets on the floor.

(Lights come up on the downstage area)

1:03—The **YOUNG LORD**, as wealthy and over-dressed as the Poet is poor, enters DL with the **DARK LADY**. She is obviously of his class, but there is something less languid and spoiled about her. The fires of this volcano are near to bursting all of the time. The Young Lord is reading her a sonnet sent to him by the adoring Poet. It is clearly nothing to the Young Lord, but the Lady is impressed. As they move R to the Poet's room she takes it from the Lord and reads it to herself.

(Downstage lights fade)

1:53—They enter the Poet's room. He greets the Lord fawningly. Clearly, the Poet's feelings for him are not entirely professional. He barely notices the Lady, who reads some of the aborted attempts which lie on the floor. The Poet presents the Lord with a ribbon-bound packet of new sonnets.

2:44—The Lady is smitten with the Poet. Call it literary lust, call it slumming...she is clearly attracted. Neither man much notices. She "accidentally" leaves her fan on the desk as she leaves with the Lord.

(Downstage lights come up)

They move back DL. The Lord treats the poems lightly. The Lady asks for them and receives them. He exits DL. She moves UL to her bedroom, places the poems on the table.

(Downstage lights fade)

She unpins her hair as her **MAID** enters UL with a floor-length dressing gown. The Maid begins to undress her.

(Lights fade on the bedroom).

3:35—The Poet finds the fan. He immediately decides to return it. He cleans himself up, puts on his best doublet, crosses DR with the fan, and moves toward the bedroom area.

(Lights come back up on the bedroom; fade on Poet's room)

The Lady is now wearing the dressing gown. She sits in the chair, reading the sonnets, as the Maid brushes her long hair for her.

4:35—The Poet enters the edge of the bedroom area. The Lady greets him warmly, thanks him for "finding" her fan. Their hands touch as she receives it. She holds his hand a beat longer than necessary. The Poet turns away, embarrassed and confused. The Maid watches knowingly. She is a little too interested. The Lady dismisses her. The Maid withdraws, but assumes a "spying" position.

5:15—The Lady approaches the Poet with the packet of sonnets. She gushes over them while maneuvering him to the bed. They sit. She caresses his face with the poems, then kisses him tenderly. He takes it, gives her a puzzled look.

(Lights up DR)

The Maid sneaks off, reappears DR with the Young Lord.

6:05—The Maid tells of the goings-on in the Lady's bedroom and is paid for it. The Poet and Lady are in a passionate embrace on the bed.

(Bedroom lights fade)

The Lord calls in a pair of seedy but competent-looking **THUGS**. He gives them instructions and money.

(DR lights fade; bedroom lights back up)

6:54—The dazed Poet is standing. He receives a ring from the smiling Lady.

(Lights up on Poet's room)

As he crosses directly to his desk and begins writing, she sits on the bed, caressing her own face with the sonnets.

(Lights fade on bedroom; come up on downstage area)

7:43—Thugs move across stage from DL, guided by the Maid, who is clearly romantically attached to one of them. She points out the Poet's room.

8:32—While the Maid waits DC, the Thugs enter the Poet's room. They start by giving him a "friendly" warning to stay away from the Lady. He refuses.

9:21—Thugs beat up the Poet, despite his heroic resistance. The Maid's lover takes the Lady's ring from his finger, gives it and a kiss to the Maid. The Thugs exit DR.

(Lights up on bedroom; the Maid moves straight to the bedroom)

10:10—Thugs appear DC, report their success to the Lord. The Lady is still on the bed. She sees her ring on the Maid's finger, questions her.

10:58—Poet recovers, arms himself with a pair of daggers, exits UR.

(Lights fade on Poet's room)

Lady grabs Maid by the hair, hurls her onto the bed. Maid resists, gets smacked down. The lady takes her ring back. The Maid runs out UL. The thugs are gleefully "re-enacting" their beating of the Poet for the Lord's amusement. The Lady strips off her dressing gown. She wears a corset, leather breeches, and thigh-high boots. She arms herself with rapier, dagger, and bullwhip and exits UL.

(Lights fade on bedroom)

11:48—The Lady enters DL, threatens the Lord. He laughs and indicates that the Thugs should show her the error of her ways. They advance on her, looking for an opening.

12:38—The Lady cooly defeats both Thugs, with extreme prejudice. They stagger off DR, bruised and bleeding. She cuts off the Lord's exit as the Poet rushes in DL, daggers drawn, to get his own revenge.

13:22—Lord draws rapier with a laugh. They fight. The Poet is defeated and in danger of imminent death.

14:15—The Lady interposes and saves the Poet. The fight gets very sexy very quickly and goes to the floor.

15:00—The Lady and Lord end up in a passionate intertwined embrace, the Lady on top. She sits up, looks at the Poet.

(Lights up on Poet's room)

He sadly retires to his desk, begins writing feverishly.

15:22—The last exuberant chords of the music. The Lord is on his back, prostrate, bullwhip around his neck. The Dark Lady is triumphantly astride him, rapier to the sky, in a red spotlight, staring at the Poet. The Poet, just as triumphantly, leaps to his feet and holds his newly-completed sonnet to the sky, in a red spotlight of his own.

(Blackout on the last note, as rapier and sonnet go up together)

RED RIDING HOOD REDUX

A play by Terry Kroenung
© 2002

SCENE: *The woods and Grandma's house.*

SET: *Almost bare. Gobos to suggest woods. Narrator DR with lectern. Grandma's house UC—a large bed, maybe a simple table, chair, and some baking items. Rolling pin is a must.*

NARRATOR is at the lectern, looking through script. She wears a long evening gown. GRANDMA is in the bed, reading a paperback romance novel—Fabio on the cover would be good. She is in typical old lady attire—housedress, kerchief. RED RIDING HOOD is pacing DL, going over her lines, smoking a cigarette. She wears a short red cape with hood (duh!), a tight miniskirt, and go-go boots. She carries the traditional basket of goodies.

<u>**NARRATOR**</u> *(to audience)*
   "Once upon a time…"

<u>**WOLF**</u> *(enters DR, behind Narrator; he wears chic black leather, wrap-around sunglasses, 2-day beard)*
   Lame!

NARRATOR
Excuse me?

WOLF
That is so lame, dude.

NARRATOR
What is?

WOLF
That bogus intro. "Once upon a time…" Here we are, 21st century…I mean, tomorrow is NOW, man…and that's the best you can come up with?

NARRATOR
I don't think you have the appropriate sensibility to properly appreciate the classic approach to a timeless work of—

WOLF
Classic? That's so yesterday. You remember Coke Classic? Battery acid in a can. Indigestible pap for the masses.

NARRATOR
Wait a minute. I happen to like rum-and—

WOLF
We are here to effect a cutting-edge deconstruction of manipulative psychosexual trash. Now hit it again. Put some balls into it this time.

NARRATOR (*after giving him a look*)
Well, I'll try, Mr.—er—?

WOLF (*hands her a card*)
Wolf. Lenny Wolf.

NARRATOR
Lenny?

WOLF
My buds call me Lazer.

NARRATOR
Lazer Wolf?

WOLF
Uh, yeah.

(*Narrator's cell phone rings; she answers*)

NARRATOR
Hello? (*nods*) Uh-huh. Yes, he did. Well, I don't really—yes, sir. Loud and clear. (*hangs up*) That was Harnick and Bock's lawyer.

WOLF
Yeah?

NARRATOR
He says one more violation of his clients' proprietary rights to *FIDDLER ON THE ROOF* and you'll be in court…getting neutered.

WOLF
Whoa! No sense of humor. See ya! (*exits SR*)

NARRATOR (*to audience*)
"Once upon a…"—no, wait. "A long time ago, in a galaxy far, far away…" (*her phone rings again; she answers*) Hello? OK, OK! Jeez, do you represent every-damn-body?

RED RIDING HOOD
Can we get on with this? You're playing hell with my story arc!

NARRATOR
Sorry! "A young virtuous maiden, pure as the driven snow, the apple of her saintly grandmother's eye…".

RED RIDING HOOD
Oy vay! Sanford Meisner, don't fail me now! (*stomps out cigarette*)

NARRATOR
"Little Red Riding Hood was taking an ill-advised shortcut through the Dark Wood of Lost Innocence, having left the Primrose Path of Triumphant Virtue—"

WOLF (*poking head out behind Narrator*)
Somebody got a grant for writing this crap?

NARRATOR
Let me get through this once, people!

WOLF/RED RIDING HOOD
Sorry!

NARRATOR
"She was on her way to her beloved Grannie's to deliver a get-well basket of cookies, chocolates, and Chivas Regal."

GRANDMA
And hurry it up, will you? I'm sinking fast!

NARRATOR
"In the midst of the fearful forest, Little Red Riding Hood encountered a dangerous creature which her innocent ways had not prepared her for".

WOLF (*enters DR, crosses to DC; in Bill Clinton mask, holding cigar*)
Hey, baby! What happened to the little blue riding hood?

RED RIDING HOOD
It's in the wash. I can't talk long, sir. I have to hurry to the humble home in Happy Hollow to deliver this basket of goodies to my sick grannie.

WOLF
  Well, far be it from me to impede a mission of mercy. Tell your grannie I feel her pain. Get along now.

RED RIDING HOOD
  Nice to have met you. (*exits UR*)

WOLF (*removes mask; admiring her backside as she moves off*)
  Goodies! Sigmund Freud...you da man! Time to visit grannie. The kindly old lost shepherd gag should work with her. (*hobbles off with floppy hat and quarterstaff, straight UC to Grannie's house; raps staff on floor*)

GRANDMA
  Is that you, dearie?

WOLF (*Teutonic accent*)
  Nein, mein frau. Ist just a lost shepherd. Can you direct me to der main road?

GRANDMA (*gets out of bed, goes up to him*)
  Why, certainly dear. It's just—(*looks at his feet*) Why, those are certainly unusual feet for a German shepherd. Not up to breed standard at all.

WOLF (*removing hat*)
  Shut up, lady! I'm all wolf!

GRANDMA (*looking him up and down*)
  Oh, yes! I can see you are! That's quite an impressive staff you're packing. You know, ever since my poor husband died in that awful fudge factory explosion all those many years ago, I've been ever so lonely.

WOLF
  Knock it off! I'm here to devour you.

GRANDMA

Fine! Just let me slip into something more—

WOLF

No, I mean that in a direct, non-metaphorical way of speaking. Sorry for the confusion.

GRANDMA

Not at all. Could you hand me that rolling pin on the table there? (*he does so*) Thank you. Such nice manners. (*screams*) Help! A ravenous wolf!

(*They fight, rolling pin vs. quarterstaff; Grandma is spry for her age; she is knocked unconscious just downstage of the bed; the wolf is about to dispatch her*)

RED RIDING HOOD (*arriving at door, knocking*)

Grannie! I'm here!

(*Wolf takes Grannie's kerchief from her head, rolls her indelicately under the bed; he jumps on bed, quarterstaff on his lap; pulls covers up to chin, puts kerchief on his head*)

WOLF

Come in, dearie!

RED RIDING HOOD

Hello, Grannie! I brought you some goodies!

WOLF

Yes, I can see you have. And you have a basket, too!

RED RIDING HOOD
Why, Grandma, your face is so hairy! Isn't your hormone replacement therapy working?

WOLF
Oh, yes, dearie. We just have to tweak the dosage, that's all.

RED RIDING HOOD
And what big eyes you have!

WOLF
A little thyroid trouble. I'll be fine.

RED RIDING HOOD
And what big teeth you have!

WOLF
New dental implants, honey. Best money I ever spent.

RED RIDING HOOD (*eyeing the prominent bulge made by the staff under the covers*)
And, Grannie, what a big—um…

WOLF (*throwing off covers and kerchief, jumping up*)
A major star like me needs a large staff. (*knocks her across the bed, jumps astride her*)

RED RIDING HOOD (*weakly*)
Help!

WOLF
Are you going to do it like that?

RED RIDING HOOD
What do you mean?

WOLF
I mean you're just going through the motions. You're not "in the moment". What's your objective? Work with me here!

RED RIDING HOOD
I'm doing my best! What about you? Are you going to "be" the wolf or just "act" the wolf?

WOLF
Oh, look who's suddenly Little Miss Equity. Don't forget who got you this job.

RED RIDING HOOD
How could I? I still have the scar on my ass from that couch spring.

NARRATOR
"And while our intrepid couple were debating the relative merits of Uta Hagen and Charles Marowitz, Red Riding Hood's piercing—if unmotivated—screams were heard by a handsome woodsman nearby. (*WOODY, in rude forester garb, with axe, appears DL*) He raced to her defense."

WOODY (*dashing into Grandma's house*)
Unhand her, you vile miscreant!

WOLF/RED RIDING HOOD
Who writes this stuff?

WOODY
My brother-in-law. Hey, he teaches middle school Language Arts! Unhand her, you vile miscreant!

WOLF (*gets off bed, twirls staff*) OK. Go ahead. Make my day. (*Narrator's phone rings*) Will you tell that guy to get a freaking life! (*to Woody*) Shall we?

(*They fight, axe vs. quarterstaff; Woody is knocked out LC; as the Wolf is about to finish him, Red Riding Hood intervenes*)

<u>RED RIDING HOOD</u>
Not this time!

<u>WOLF</u>
See, that was good. I **<u>BELIEVED</u>** that!

<u>RED RIDING HOOD</u> (*giggles*)
Thanks!

<u>WOLF</u>
You really think you can kick my ass, little girl?

<u>RED RIDING HOOD</u>
The fight director practically guaranteed it.

(*They fight; Red Riding Hood is VERY acrobatic; midway through the fight, she uses the rolling pin in one hand and the axe in the other; the Wolf falls, stunned, DC; Red Riding Hood helps Woody to the bed; they both sit*)

<u>RED RIDING HOOD</u>
Thank you for helping me. Are you all right?

<u>WOODY</u>
I think so. Where's your Grannie?

<u>GRANNIE</u> (*head pokes out from under bed, between their feet*)
Trying to get out from under this bed, which would be a lot easier if you'd both lose some weight!

<u>WOODY/RED RIDING HOOD</u> (*jumping up*)
Sorry!

<u>GRANNIE</u> (*standing*)
Hello, dearie. Sorry about the mess.

RED RIDING HOOD
Oh, Grannie! I hope that awful wolf didn't do anything to you.

GRANNIE (*sighs*)
Not a damned thing. Ah, there he is.

WOODY (*picks up axe*)
I'll take care of him.

GRANNIE
No, no! Just toss him on my bed. I'll make sure he's...punished...later.

RED RIDING HOOD
You're sure?

GRANNIE
Trust me, he'll be howling for mercy before I'm done with him. You two run along now. I have to get started on teaching him some discipline.

RED RIDING HOOD
All right, then. I'll check up on you tomorrow.

GRANNIE
That'll be fine, dearie. (*takes a riding crop from under her pillow*) Make sure you knock first.

RED RIDING HOOD (*walking DR with Woody*)
I never asked you your name.

WOODY (*carrying Wolf's staff*)
Woody.

RED RIDING HOOD
Oh, really? You know, I have a feeling this is the beginning of a beautiful friendship.

(*they exit DR; Narrator's phone rings again*)

<u>NARRATOR</u>
  Aw, Jeez!

(*BLACKOUT*)

DEATH SONG

A play by Terry Kroenung
© 2002

<u>SCENE</u>—*The sacred circle of the Amazons.*

<u>SET</u>—*Bare stage. Circle in center defined by light only. Out of view UC is a raised platform where Artemis will later appear.*

*MOLPADIA, a girl just turned 18, is fighting **ANTIANEIRA**, a strong woman in her late 20's. They use short swords and bucklers. Their dress is simple tunics and sandals. No armor is worn. Their hair is loose. This is a "friendly" match.*
    Drums and flutes are providing a driving rhythm to the fight, which is underway as the lights come up. Music builds as the fight builds.
    Molpadia is flashy, cocky, tries too hard. She seems less friendly and relaxed about the fight than her opponent, who is clean, precise, focused. Antianeira ends up putting the younger woman down and forces her to yield. Music stops.

<u>ANTIANEIRA</u>
You've bettered yourself.

<u>MOLPADIA</u>
And lost.

18

ANTIANEIRA
But you lasted twice as long this time.

MOLPADIA
And lost! *(ignores her outstretched hand, rises on her own; starts to walk off L)*

ANTIANEIRA
Molpadia! *(Molpadia stops, but does not turn to her)* Observe the forms, please.

MOLPADIA *(turning; in a surly tone)*
Always the forms. Never the substance. *(Antianeira waits her out; Molpadia makes a cursory salute)* "Blood and iron", my Lady Antianeira.

ANTIANEIRA *(returning salute smartly)*
"The moon kisses all." Go now. Clean up for prayers.

(Molpadia stalks off L. **PENTHESILEA**, *a strong woman in her early 30's, has appeared from DL)*

PENTHESILEA
Her skills are progressing remarkably.

ANTIANEIRA
But her heart is mired in pride.

PENTHESILEA
It may take a full team to pull free. That's why she has a mentor.

ANTIANEIRA
I'm afraid the team is not working together in the harness.

PENTHESILEA
Yet. Don't give up on your apprentice too easily.

ANTIANEIRA
I haven't. But I'm sorely tempted to use the whip on this stubborn calf.

PENTHISILEA
We should go gently with this one. Foundlings are different from native-born Amazons. No shared parentage or history...constant questioning and testing...taking longer to feel a part of the tribe...

ANTIANEIRA
If they ever do.

PENTHESILEA
You have to help that to happen. How is she doing in her other lessons, besides combat?

ANTIANEIRA
Oh, she's sharp as a new blade—when she's in the mood. But it seems she mostly marks time until fight class.

PENTHESILEA
Hmmm. And who might she remind us of in that?

ANTIANEIRA (*smiles*)
But I grew out of it.

PENTHESILEA
Only after I dragged you, kicking and screaming.

ANTIANEIRA (*shrugs*)
That's how we enter the world.

PENTHESILEA
And how most of us leave it.

ANTIANEIRA
I only hope the Fates have given her a long time to wait for that.

PENTHESILEA
None of us gets to choose the—

ANTIANEIRA
Really? But we do choose our battle names.

PENTHESILEA
I remember when you announced yours at council. Just her age, too.

PENTHESILEA/ANTIANEIRA
"Antianeira will I be...know that it means 'Against the sea'!"

PENTHESILEA
Cheeky bitch.

ANTIANEIRA
We all thought we could pummel Poseidon in that class.

PENTHESILEA
I remember you having too much wine and giving it a try.

ANTIANEIRA
That was a very tiny boat! Thanks for pulling me out. Were you ever that way?

PENTHESILEA
I chose <u>Penthesilea</u> for a battle name!

PENTHESILEA/ANTIANEIRA
"Compelling men to mourn"!

ANTIANEIRA
She's already chosen her name, you know.

PENTHESILEA
Has she? And...?

ANTIANEIRA
Molpadia.

PENTHESILEA
Ahh…"Death Song". Presumably that of her enemies.

ANTIANEIRA
One hopes. But there's a darkness to this one that worries me. A brooding about her unknown parentage. She seems adrift, out of sight of land, on the wine-dark sea. As quick to anger as a shaken wasp's nest…

PENTHESILEA
Try to channel it. The rest of us will help.

ANTIANEIRA
Thank you. You'll need to. And now I'd better help her get ready for prayers.

PENTHESILEA
I need to do the same for Hippolyta. "Blood and iron."

ANTIANEIRA
"The moon kisses all."

(*Penthesilea exits UR; ANTIANEIRA exits DL; Molpadia enters UL, in white robe and silver head circlet; she stops in the center of the circle of light, kneels*)

MOLPADIA
Great Lady of the Moon, hear your humble daughter. I am grateful for the home you've given me here, for the sisters who've taken me in. If the Fates were to measure my life to a thousand years, I could never repay you…nor them.

But I feel like a thorn in a tender breast…causing pain with every breath. And suffering the same. I'm out of place. Are those truly hateful stares I feel from all I pass, or do I merely dream them? No mother, no father, no city. Living on the good graces of these great women…like a stray cat no one wants, but which obligation forbids killing.

Who am I? Child of light, or child of storm? Spawned by love, or spawned by rage? Why do I seek to embrace the one, but end up consummating with the other? What god drives me to clutch my sword, even at the smiles of my sisters? What is this pernicious anger that devours my soul?

Great Lady of the Silver Bow, Artemis, Huntress Supreme…help me to a destiny before this flame consumes me! Clear my path to you…send me an omen, a sign…a token of your favor. Whatever it may be, I shall accept it, rather than drown in this terrible unknowing. I will take my assigned road, whether it lead to wisdom or folly.

(Flute music begins, soft and reverent, with slow muffled drums underneath. Penthesilea, Antianeira, and **HIPPOLYTA**, *Queen of Amazons, enter from DR, DL, and UC respectively. They are dressed like Molpadia. They take triangular positions around the circle, with Molpadia DC. Antianeira holds a strange long sword in both hands, horizontally)*

HIPPOLYTA *(handsome, regal; in her mid-30's; she holds a chalice)*
Great Lady of the Moon, hear your humble daughter. Drink of our prayers. bathe in our love, as we bathe in yours. Silver us with your strength.

*(**ARTEMIS** is revealed by silvery light, UC on raised platform; she is beautiful and powerful at the same time; she wears a simple white tunic, head circlet, and carries a silver bow)*

ARTEMIS
Who calls to the Huntress? Who sings to my ancient soul?

HIPPOLYTA
Hippolyta, She of the Stampeding Horses…Queen of Amazons.

ARTEMIS
I see a shadow in your sacred circle. A cloud passes before the face of the moon.

HIPPOLYTA
Where is this cloud, Huntress?

ARTEMIS
Before you.

(*Lights dim slightly, leaving Molpadia in an ironic spot of brightness*)

ANTIANEIRA
My apprentice is troubled, Lady. (*walks to center of circle with sword*)

ARTEMIS
My brother troubles her…to her great misery, I fear.

PENTHESILEA
The Lord Apollo?

ARTEMIS
No. Hold the sword up to my light. The sword you found on her bed, as if from nowhere.

(*Antianeira holds the sword over her head. A red light surrounds her*)

HIPPOLYTA
Where did it come from, Lady?

ARTEMIS
My brother forged it…for his bastard daughter. Ares, God of War…Lord of Battle.

MOLPADIA *(steps forward)*
My father? *(reaches for sword)*

ARTEMIS *(stepping down, entering top of circle; Amazons kneel)*
Accept your token…

(Molpadia grasps sword; drums quicken; she is bathed in red light)

ARTEMIS
…And embrace your folly.

(Molpadia begins to sing. It is a haunting, wordless keening, notes that are terrifying and terrified at the same time. It builds for the rest of the play, broken only by her occasional pleadings. The sword takes on a life of its own, possessing Molpadia completely. She spins, whirls, goes through an elaborate attack/defense sequence similar to an Asian kata. The perplexed Amazons move away from her, to the edge of the circle. Artemis has returned to her lighted position atop the UC platform. She makes all the same moves as Mopadia, using her bow, as if she is a grim puppeteer. Music builds in speed and intensity, then stops. Molpadia and Artemis freeze)

ARTEMIS
Daughters…arm yourselves. Her path is paved by Ares, and can end only in blood and iron…unkissed by the moon.

(Amazons exit quickly, as Molpadia and Artemis resume their previous movements, only more quickly. Hippolyta returns first, in the simple Amazon tunic, with a sword. She fights with Molpadia, who does all the attacking. Hippolyta is obviously reluctant)

MOLPADIA

Help me, Your Grace! I can't stop it!

HIPPOLYTA

Throw the cursed sword away, child!

(Molpadia tries three times to hurl the sword across the stage, punctuated by drums. The sword will not leave her hand. Her song resumes, and the sword impels her toward Hippolyta again)

MOLPADIA

I'm so sorry!

HIPPOLYTA

Lady of the Silver Bow…Help her!

ARTEMIS

Her cord has been measured. Even the gods must bend to the will of Fate.

(The fight resumes, this time with Hippolyta reluctantly attacking. Penthesilea enters with 2 short swords, and it becomes a two-on-one duel, with Molpadia using sword, hand, and foot with incredible speed)

HIPPOLYTA

Grab her and hold her! I'll try to pull the sword from her hand!

(Penthesilea tries to bear hug Molpadia, but is sent flying across the circle, stunned)

MOLPADIA
Forgive me, my sister!

ANTIANEIRA *(rushing into the circle with sword and buckler)*
No, child…forgive ME!

(She attacks Molpadia savagely, holding nothing back. Hippolyta attacks the same way. Molpadia's eerie singing continues)

MOLPADIA *(to the heavens)*
What sin have I committed?!

ARTEMIS
You are mortal. Suffering is your birthright.

MOLPADIA
But my father is—

ARTEMIS
—In the sword, child. Pray to him. But hope not. He is what he is.

(The fighting and singing continue at a frantic pace, to appropriate music. The feeling should be of Bacchic frenzy. Penthesilea recovers, rejoins the fight with a spear. It is now an incredible four-way combat, with Artemis still pantomiming all of Molpadia's moves with her bow)

MOLPADIA *(sings this)*
Father—!! *(Hipployta falls from a kick)*
Father—!! *(Penthesilea falls from a pommel punch)*
Father—!! *(Antianeira falls from a bind)*

(Molpadia is dead center, still singing, still in a red light from above. The sword points straight up into the light, as if of its own will. The red light vanishes, replaced by backlight only. The Amazons recover and stab her simultaneously. Molpadia shrieks. Music stops)

MOLPADIA
—Why have you...begotten me?

(She falls dead. Blackout)

ASSAIL! ASSAIL!

A play by Terry Kroenung
© 2002

SCENE: *Bloomingdale's (or somewhere similar). The morning after Thanksgiving.*

SET: *Picked-over garment racks, plastic and wooden hangers swaying. A couple of mostly-empty bargain bins. A lonely mannequin or two. A tall hat rack. The odd piece of discarded clothing on the floor.*

*EUNICE and **MYRTLE** browse down left. Not old, not young. Worn out from a long day of bargain battles. They are professionals at this. **RITA** and **JATONYA** enter up right. Young, hip, "too cool" to be here. **WAYNE**, a crisply-dressed sales assistant, is at center trying to create order out of the chaotic displays.*

Jatonya

So I told that boy, if he was gonna act like that, he could just get his lazy, but admittedly fine, chocolate ass out from under my $300 Scandanavian goose down duvet and go find hisself a job.

Rita

Amen to that, sister.

Jatonya

I said, "I may have woke up next to you without knowin' your name, but damn! This woman deserves respect!"

Rita

Me and Julio went through the same thing. He was all puffed-up about how he had himself a **busload** of bitches, and I was just "Tuesday" to him.

Jatonya

And so?

Rita

And so I locked him naked out on the fire escape.

Jatonya

You go, girl!

Rita

Just as all the school busses were goin' by.

Jatonya

Wooo!

Rita

He's bangin' on the slidin' door, hollerin': "Come, on, Rita! At least gimme sumpin' to wear while the kids are lookin'!"

Jatonya

And your instant reply was—?

Rita

Threw him my pink baby doll nightie with the marabou stork trim.

Rita/Jatonya

"$49.95, one size fits most"!

(They slap hands and giggle, hunting through a bin)

Eunice
So, how's your mother?

Myrtle
Better.

Eunice
Better?

Myrtle
Better call the mortician, she's not long for this world.

Eunice
How long's she been sick?

Myrtle
1949. And your darling husband?

Eunice
Ah...touch-and-go.

Myrtle
Sounds like my first honeymoon.

Eunice
Sounds like my last doctor's visit.

Myrtle
So, Eunice, are the kids home from college?

Eunice
Well, their laundry is. I haven't spotted **them** yet.

Myrtle
I sympathize. The only thing dirtier than my Harvey's clothes is his mind.

Eunice
Sometimes I wonder what they're teaching them at those fancy-schmancy medical schools.

Myrtle
No, Harvey's in law school at Columbia.

Eunice
Oh. Well, there you have it.

(Rita and Jatonya have migrated to center)

Rita *(to Wayne; she holds a sweater)*
'Scuse me. Do you have this in a size 2?

Wayne *(looking her up and down)*
Shopping for your Barbie doll collection?

(Rita immediately slaps him upside his head)

Wayne
I'd be delighted to check in the back for you. *(exits up left)*

Rita
Jeez, if I was shoppin' for abuse I coulda stayed home with Julio.

Jatonya *(imitating store announcer)*
"Attention, please! We are now offering huge discounts on ridicule, for a limited time only."

Rita
"Invective now half-off."

Jatonya *(eyes her as if she's from Mars)*
Invective?

Rita
I'm goin' to night school. So sue me.

(Wayne comes back with a sweater)

Wayne
Will a 10 do?

Rita *(takes it)*
Deal.

(Wayne returns to organizing. Rita and Jatonya move left as Eunice and Myrtle amble to down center)

Eunice
So I said to her, I said, "Gladys, Mrs. Fishbein's son just this week got back from his Doctors Without Borders trip. You need to put that darling daughter of yours in her best dress and march her right down to their apartment with a bowl of matzoh ball soup, before some **other** mother finds out there's an unmarried podiatrist in the building. 14 is most definitely **not** too early to be laying the groundwork."

Myrtle
Doctors Without Borders. A great organization.

Eunice
But doctors without wives—

Myrtle/Eunice
—is a crying shame.

(Wayne picks up a red silk scarf from the floor and drapes it around the neck of a mannequin, up center)

Rita *(poking Jatonya)*
   Hey, Jatonya!

Eunice *(poking Myrtle)*
   Myrtle!

Jatonya
   Ohhh! I would look so good in that! *(moves toward the scarf)*

Rita
   Maybe so, but I spied it first. *(moves toward the scarf)*

Eunice
   I can get a mint for that on E-Bay! *(moves toward the scarf)*

Myrtle
   Only when you pry it from my cold, dead fingers! *(moves toward the scarf)*

Eunice
   Careful what you wish for!

(All four shoppers stalk the scarf slowly, like lionesses creeping up on a herd of antelope. Wayne is backed up against the mannequin in terror; he's been here before)

Wayne
   Ladies! Ladies! Please! I have an invalid husband to support!

(Rita lunges for the scarf, but Jatonya grabs her by the neck and flings her stage right, into a garment rack. As Jatonya turns to grasp the scarf, Eunice arrives, head butts her, and grabs one end of the scarf. Myrtle grabs the other. Wayne is tangled between them)

Eunice
Let go!

Myrtle
Why? Do I have "schmuck" written on my forehead?

Wayne
Do I have "organ donor" written on mine?

(Rita picks up a long piece of the broken garment rack, wields it as a quarterstaff. Jatonya picks up a pair of wooden clothes hangers, one in each hand. Eunice, Myrtle, and Wayne move down left as a unit)

Rita
What you mean, sucker-punching me?

Jatonya
A hard bargain knows no conscience!

(They fight, stage right. At stage left, Wayne is spun toward center stage, where he hides in a bin. Eunice and Myrtle keep hold of the scarf. Myrtle jerks on it, Eunice lurches into her knee, belly-first, and drops. Myrtle wraps the scarf loosely around her own neck As she tries to rush for the up right exit, Rita and Jatonya stop fighting and bar her way)

Rita
My name is Rita Elena Montano. You stole my scarf. Prepare to die.

(She attacks. Myrtle dives under the center bin as Wayne peeps out the top. He shrieks as he almost loses his head. Myrtle grabs the hat rack and confronts Rita down right. Eunice has recovered. She holds a wooden hanger in one hand and a mannequin as a shield in the other. She stands beside Myrtle. Jatonya takes her place beside Rita)

Eunice
Once more, unto the bitch, dear friend!

Jatonya
God for Armani, Giorgio, and St. Laurent!

(Everyone charges. Rita and Myrtle fight down right, Eunice and Jatonya fight up left. Wayne cautiously exits the bin with a handful of identical red scarves, which he casually drapes decoratively on the up center display as the lights fade out)

THORNS

A play by Terry Kroenung
© 2002

SCENE: *Macbeth's castle of Dunsinane, mid-11th century.*

SET: *A richly-appointed open hall. Entrances up left and up right. Embroidered carpets on the floor. Weapons hung on the upstage wall in heraldic displays. A large table up center, with 2 chairs. An impressive bouquet of roses dominates the table.*

*(**THREE YOUNG WOMEN** stand before the table, dressed well but not gaudily. The middle one holds a rudely-fashioned doll about a foot tall. It resembles a man in battle array. They whisper to themselves for a moment)*

Woman 1 *(at center, with doll)*
  Is the likeness fair enough?

Woman 2 *(stage right of her)*
  'Twill serve.

Woman 3 *(stage left of center)*
  The living image in miniature.

Woman 1
  He is strong. This will go hard, I think.

Woman 2

They are strong alike.

Woman 3

Hush! She is here.

*(Woman 1 hastily tucks the doll away. **GRUOCH** enters up right. She is in her early to mid-20's, attractive, dressed like nobility. She nods to them as they curtsey and move to stage left. She paces down center, reading a letter to herself)*

Gruoch *(reading aloud)*

"Fear not that I use my dread office to command your obedience in this matter. Think of me merely as a fond old man who wants to see the gleam of happiness in the bright eyes of his foster daughter. A king who wields his scepter as a cudgel to drive his subjects into Cupid's arms is a shallow ruler.

The lord Macbeth needs no such aid. His worth is evident to all who meet him. He is my good sword arm, the shield of our fair state. We live free from fear thanks to his incessant valor. But do not think that I am foisting upon you some bloodthirsty ogre who would rather butcher a foe than kiss a hand. He is a gentleman in all seasons, as famous for his diplomacy as for his savagery in battle. Elegant in manner, word, and thought. When we hold a dance at court he is always the last to quit the floor, loath to disappoint the battalions of ladies who seek his favor. I did with mine own eyes spy him giving secret aid to an orphaned beggar child last Michaelmas eve, with no more thought of any recompense or renown for the deed than the eagle gives to the dove. In short, my almost-daughter, the man is worth a glance.

Moreover, he is besotted with you. To tell you truly, this is partly from my descanting on your charms ad nauseum. 'Gruoch this and Gruoch-that', I tell him. I fear I make of you a sister to Diana and Athena. Set it down to my fond conceit. All I ask is the boon of your attending to his suit. If you like not his fair face, fairer form, and fairest soul, nothing more will be said. He awaits your arrival at Dunsinane for Yule.

Yours in love, whatever your decision…Duncan, King of Scotland." *(She hands the letter to Woman 1)* The man grows more to rival Apollo with every new reading of that letter.

Woman 1

Our good king would surely never spread a layer of gold upon a mongrel just to deceive you, m'lady.

Gruoch

Oh, perhaps not with hard intent. But often our will is servant to our hidden desire.

(Woman 2 giggles. Woman 3 elbows her)

Gruoch *(rolling her eyes at this)*

Duncan is a king. He has family alliances, estates, and treaties to think of. Consideration of them simmers like a bog beneath all his words and deeds. Let us never lose sight of the fact.

Woman 3

But you are his Fairy Princess, he always says.

Gruoch

But not a Prince. *(pause)* I am a woman. You would do well to remember who we are…and where we are.

Woman 1 *(fussing over her)*

We are in a great lord's house, m'lady. A lord who may become **your** lord very soon.

Gruoch *(wryly)*

My lord.

Woman 2
A lord who is handsome, strong, and—

Woman 3
—And rich.

Woman 1
And you are the king's favorite. Few women in the realm would weep at your predicament, m'lady.

Gruoch
My predicament...an orphan girl, raised at the sovereign's sufferance, treated as a lapdog, then handed off to his friend like a party favor—

Macbeth *(entering up right)*
You prize yourself too lightly, my lady Gruoch.

(Women start at his sudden words)

Gruoch *(curtseying)*
My lord Macbeth.

Macbeth *(crossing to her)*
A blessed Yule gift from the gods, perhaps, but never a mere party favor. *(kisses her hand)*

Gruoch
You honor me, sir.

Macbeth
Oh, no. It is you who honor me...riding all this way in the snow to hear stammering love rhymes in a musty old fortress.

Gruoch
Musty? Perhaps. I would have to take you at your word for that. Who could tell with every chamber awash in roses? *(smelling them)*

How on earth do you grow them here in winter? A little sorcery in the off-season?

Macbeth (*smiling*)
More prosaic than that, I'm afraid. I have a Frenchman gardener who makes them thrive under glass atop the south tower. I spend nearly every afternoon up there. Cutting off blossoms pleases me more than cutting off heads…contrary to my reputation.

Gruoch
Without your skill at the former we might have precious little opportunity to enjoy the bounty of the latter.

Macbeth
Lamentably so. It is a thorny world. But I hardly fight alone.

Gruoch
Truly spoken. Yet you live alone. A valiant thane, honored above all other men in Scotland, yet with no lady by his side. A choice to wonder at.

Macbeth (*pause*)
Not entirely by choice.

Gruoch
My lord?

Macbeth (*escorting her to the stage left chair*)
I would not have you buy the proverbial pig in a poke.

Gruoch (*smiling*)
No one could rightly consider you such a—

Macbeth
Please. Permit me. (*pause*) At my birth there was fire in the sky. My father, astonished at such an omen, begged a seer to explain the event, for good or for ill, but truly. She prophesied that my mother

would pass before the full moon…and any woman I married would die with blood on her hands, raving.

Gruoch *(catching her breath)*
And your mother—?

Macbeth
Died of plague.

Gruoch
Oh! I'm so—

Macbeth
Ten years later.

Gruoch *(eyes wide)*
Then the prophecy was—

Macbeth
Not quite accurate.

Gruoch
Well, soothsayers and astrologers are rarely…entirely…so.

Macbeth
She breathed her last on the day before a full moon. My grieving father pointed out that the seer had not specified in her prophecy precisely **which** full moon. Before my mother's final sigh had ceased to echo in the chamber, he swore me to eternal celibacy, that I might be spared the curse that had befallen him.

Gruoch
I marvel, then, that you and I are arrived at this meeting.

Macbeth
You may well do so. I assure you, I would not be here if I were still of the mind that the prophecy still hunted true. I have sought out countless astrologers, prophets, seers—yes, even witches—in order to learn the value of their predictions. What I have come to

believe is that you, or I, or your lovely handmaidens there *(women giggle)* could divine the future as efficaciously as most practitioners of the black arts.

Gruoch *(standing)*
  Then your oath is broken?

Macbeth
  I told my father so as he lay dying. They may have been the last words to reach his sad tired ears.

Gruoch
  So here we stand…a brace of orphans.

Macbeth *(stroking her cheek)*
  Mayhap…a new mother and father. Someday.

Gruoch
  I blush, sir.

Macbeth
  It only adds to your beauty.

Gruoch
  I do not color because of your words, my lord, but because I, too, have sworn an oath. One I dare not break.

Macbeth
  I would never ask it of you. What is it?

Gruoch
  Despite the fine feminine gown you see me in, I must tell you that I was quite the tomboy as a young girl. Climbing trees. Catching frogs. Handily defeating all the boys in contests at arm wrestling and spitting…

Macbeth
  Many a gawky girl, now a graceful lady, might say the same.

Gruoch

The king saw me one afternoon, after I had pinned both his scrawny sons, Malcolm and Donalbain, to the ground and rubbed cow manure in their faces. He laughed, held me to his breast, and said it would take a strong man to win me and keep me. I perfectly recall laughing with him, and declaring that I would remain a maid to the end of my days, unless I found a great hero who could tame me. That night I swore the same on a falling star over Inverness.

Macbeth (*to himself*)

Fire in the sky…

Gruoch

So, shall we have a spitting contest, my lord? (*looks about*) No, the appointments of the hall are much too costly. Arm wrestling? (*strokes his arm*) No, the seams might split on your fine raiment. (*sees sword display*) Ah! Perhaps a genteel dance in steel?

Macbeth (*appalled*)

My lady, I dare not!

Gruoch

Tut! Where's the harm, sir? (*draws swords*)

Macbeth

In your lovely flesh, if this miscarry.

Gruoch

Miscarry? You talk like frightened bride (*walks up very close to him*) I do not fear your weapon. I am well-taught. (*brings sword handle up between them, pommel-first, puts it in his hand*)

Macbeth

I like this not. I have many a scar from practicing this in deadly earnest, while you—

Gruoch
    —Have never been touched. *(pulls his face to hers)* Besides, who says this is not in deadly earnest? *(bites his ear)* Be at ease. I shall not tell the king.

Macbeth
    If you lie dead, my lady, **I** must needs tell him.

Gruoch
    If I were to…die, I would fain have it at your hands, brave Macbeth. *(quick kiss)* Lay on!

(She pushes him away suddenly, launches a cut at his head, which he just manages to parry)

Macbeth *(a whisper)*
    May the gods guide my hand.

(They fight with spirit. Gruoch does most of the attacking. They go over, around, and under the furniture, scatter the women, and use every inch of the stage. Gruoch is having a wonderful time. Eventually the fight ends down center, with her on her back, defeated but not disarmed. Macbeth straddles her, clearly thankful that she—and he, truth be told—is not hurt)

Gruoch *(running a hand teasingly up his leg)*
    See? Not a scratch.

Macbeth *(pulling her to her feet; she ends up full-front against him)*
    Save on my heart.

Gruoch *(pause; moving to the table)*
    Did I score, then?

Macbeth *(following her; pulls rose from vase)*
Can you doubt it? *(offers rose to her)*

(Gruoch clasps both her hands around his hand; slowly, deliberately, with a thin smile she squeezes until his face betrays that the thorns are piercing his palm)

Gruoch
More battle scars, my thane. My love. *(long kiss, hands still clasped tightly)* My husband. *(motions to Woman 3, who gives her a white handkerchief; Gruoch dips it in the vase water, starts to clean his wounds)* They will tell legends about us until **all** of the stars do fall.

Macbeth
And the moon, too…my lady Macbeth.

(She finishes cleaning his hand; she dips the handkerchief in the vase again and begins washing his blood from her own hands)

Gruoch
Foolish prophecies…*(keeps washing)* What do witches know…? *(keeps washing)* How can the puny planets reign over the lives of such as us…? *(still washing)* We will make our own destiny, my lord.

Macbeth *(grasping her hands)*
They are quite clean, my…love.

Gruoch *(smiling)*
So they are. *(gives bloody handkerchief back to Woman 3)*

Macbeth
I go to write the king, to praise his matchmaking skill. *(kisses her hands)*

Gruoch
Send all my love to my foster father. *(long kiss; during the kiss, she rubs her hands)* Well, nearly all.

(Macbeth exits up right; Gruoch turns to her women)

Woman 2
M'lady will be a thane's wife!

Woman 1
Dunsinane is your palace now!

Woman 3
I'll wager you have captured his very soul!

Gruoch *(smiles thinly)*
'Tis a good beginning. *(starts out up left)* Attend me in my chamber. I feel I need…a bath. *(exits)*

(Women gather at the table. Woman 1 produces the doll again. Woman 3 wraps the bloody handkerchief around it. Woman 2 plucks a rose from the vase, strips it of its petals. She wraps the thorny stem around the doll and ties it in a knot. All three women spit on the doll. They then clasp hands around the table, with the doll standing upright on it)

Woman 1
When shall we three meet again?

Woman 2
In thunder…

Woman 3
…Lightning…

<u>All Three Women</u>
   …Or in rain!

(Thunder; spot on women; blackout)

SURRENDER, DOROTHY

A play by Terry Kroenung
© 2002

<u>SCENE</u>: *Construction site, lunchtime*

<u>SET</u>: *Scaffold up center to suggest a job site. Pile of lumber, various sizes, including plywood, DR. Trash can with lid DL, along with plastic PVC pipe. Sawhorses UC. Hammers, crowbars, and other tools are scattered about.*

DOROTHY, EMILY, GLINDA, *and* **WIZZIE** *sit on the scaffold, eating lunch and occasionally hooting at male passersby.*

<u>Dorothy</u> *(has her lunch in a covered basket)*
This blows. I mean, this really **<u>sucks</u>**!

<u>Glinda</u>
Make up your mind.

<u>Emily</u>
You kiss your mother with that mouth?

<u>Dorothy</u>
Yeah, and sometimes I give her a little—*(wags tongue at her)*

Glinda

I don't wanna know.

Wizzie

You still bitchin' 'bout the party?

Dorothy

Yeah, I'm still bitchin' 'bout the party. Gonna keep on bitchin', too.

Glinda

And this'll change things exactly—how?

Emily

Glenda, dear, you simply do not comprehend the gestalt of bitching.

Wizzie (*to male passerby*)

Woo-hoo! Buns o' steel!

Glinda

Hey, cupcake, come here and I'll polish those for ya—with my ankles!

Dorothy

Gestalt? Do you have any idea what that even means? One community college class and suddenly yer Sigmund Freakin' Freud?

Emily

No, one fully-functioning brain and I'm a decent human being. You should try it sometime.

Dorothy

You know what, Little Miss Emily, one of these days—

Emily

Why, you can count! Isn't that sweet?

Dorothy
Bite me.

Glinda
Dorothy, all your whinin' is gonna do is give you a early heart attack. That's what happened to my Bert. Nothin' but negativity mornin', noon, and night. Now he's at Beth Israel getting' a forward pass.

Emily
BYpass, dearie.

Glinda
Huh?

Emily
BY. BY.

Glinda
Where ya goin'?

Dorothy
Yer dumber' a bag o' hammers, you know that?

Wizzie
Aw, leave her alone. Just 'cause you're pissed off at Frank don't mean you hafta take it out on us.

Glinda
Yeah! Wasn't me scheduled a stag party on a workday.

Dorothy
A **Friday**, no less.

Wizzie
Yeah, yeah. So what? He's the boss, he can do what he wants.

Glinda (*smirking*)
Or who he wants.

<u>Dorothy</u>
What's that s'posed t' mean?

<u>Glinda</u> *(quick glance at Wizzie)*
Oh...nothin'.

<u>Emily</u>
Dorothy, dear, you are in need of a refresher course on the Essential Characteristics of the Modern Male.

<u>Dorothy</u>
I know all I need to know—Frank's a prick.

(Wizzie giggles, then quickly stifles it)

<u>Emily</u>
That's the elementary course. This is the advanced. Lesson One—All men have two brains. And they cannot function simultaneously.

<u>Dorothy</u>
Duh!

<u>Emily</u>
When the more southerly brain is active, the blood supply is rerouted from the upper brain.

<u>Wizzie</u> *(spying another male passerby)*
Hi, baby! *(makes kissing sounds)*

<u>Glinda</u>
Honey, a package like that needs a Federal Express truck!

<u>Emily</u>
When the northern brain is engaged, the other one slumbers...but is ever-vigilant.

Wizzie *(poking through her lunchbox)*
Man, I can never get a good fork.

Glinda *(half whisper)*
Not what I heard.

Wizzie *(glancing at Dorothy)*
Ssshh!

Emily
Your darling husband, Frank, our sainted employer, has engaged the clutch—so to speak—on his lower mechanism; thus, he is taking your only begotten son, Ray, out for his 21st birthday party. Predictably, this soiree is occurring, even as we speak, at a neighboring salon of exotique terpsichore.

Dorothy *(after a pause)*
What in the **hell** did you just say?

Emily *(sighs)*
They left us here so they could stuff cash into G-strings at Madame Medusa's. Jeez!

Dorothy
I know that! No big deal.

Glinda
Then **what** is your problem?

Dorothy
The problem is that **we** have to work while they're off oglin' implants!

Wizzie
No, the problem is that he picked the strip club where you two met.

Glinda
I think it's kinda sweet.

Dorothy
Wizzie, spare me the 25-cent analysis.

Emily
Get over it. If you don't know what to expect from Frank after a quarter-century of wedded bliss—

Dorothy *(snorts)*
Bliss! Rhymes with—

Wizzie *(eyeing male passerby)*
—Pistol-Packin' Peter!

Glinda
Take the safety off that cannon and fire at will, babe!

Dorothy
Will you two put a sock in it! And while yer at it, shut your mouths, too.

Glinda
Quit bein' such a witch, Dorothy! Just because you can't keep Frank at home—

(Wizzie punches her in the arm)

Dorothy
What's that s'posed to mean? *(looks at Wizzie)* Ah…

Glinda
You know what they say: "There's no place like home!"

Wizzie
She doesn't know what she's talkin'—

Emily
Come on, everyone. Time to get back to work. Grab your tools.

Dorothy
   Looks like someone's already grabbed **mine**.

(They hop off the scaffold and scatter to their jobs. Wizzie moves DR, Dorothy and Glinda go DL. Emily moves to C to look at blueprints)

Dorothy *(low voice, to Glinda)*
   All right, Glinda, give.

Glinda
   What?

Dorothy
   You can't keep a secret to save your Mama's life. What's up with Wizzie and Frank?

(Their voices subside, but the conversation continues quietly and intensely)

Emily
   Wizzie, we need to get those 2 x 4's cut.

Wizzie
   OK.

Emily
   And bring that crowbar when you come.

Wizzie *(holding it up—one of the long ones)*
   This one?

Emily
   That's it.

(Dorothy lets out a roar and grabs Glinda by the hair. She hurls her toward C)

Dorothy
I knew it! *(points at Wizzie)* I'm gonna fall on you like a two-story house, missy!

Emily
Now, let's not get—

Dorothy
You stay outta this! *(to Wizzie)* Yer cover's blown, honey. Madame Brain-Trust here blabbed the whole thing. *(advances to C)* I knew that you jumped everything with a fly, but couldn't you leave my husband alone?

Wizzie
You got it backwards.

Dorothy *(laughs)*
Oh, I suppose he was all over **you**, huh?

Wizzie
Like white on rice. At your mama's wedding.

Dorothy *(stops)*
That was eight years ago!

Wizzie *(shrugs)*
Guess ya shoulda had a crystal ball to keep track of him.

Dorothy
I'm gonna break his crystal balls. He never could keep his winkie under control. But first...I'm so gonna mess you up.

Wizzie
Better bring some help. And some bandages.

(They fight at C: Wizzie's crowbar vs. Dorothy's hammer and screwdriver. Emily tries to break it up, but is hurled DL. She grabs the trash can lid as a shield and a 3-foot piece of pipe as a weapon. Glinda crawls DR and grabs a 2 x 4 for protection. The fight becomes a vigorous 3-way affair as Emily tries to intervene again. It moves upstage amongst and atop the scaffolding, then moves back to C. Wizzie is flung DR into Glinda. The other pair continues to fight LC)

Wizzie
Thanks a lot, ya little narc!

Glinda
I didn't mean to!

Wizzie *(punches her)*
Sorry, I didn't mean to do that, either.

Glinda
I'm gonna knock yer ass from here to Kansas!

Wizzie *(displaying fist)*
Not before I show you my white tornado!

(They fight. General melee ensues. Eventually every item on stage—including an oil can and an axe—is used, everyone has fought everyone else, and they are all sprawled about the stage, stunned and exhausted; the last move involves Glinda throwing water in Dorothy's face)

Dorothy
Thanks a lot, Ding-Dong! *(sags; all the fight is out of her now)*

Glinda
Aw…isn't that your pet name for Frank?

Dorothy
'Pet' bein' the operative word. When I get home I'm gonna neuter him.

Emily
I would observe it's somewhat late in the day to be suddenly so concerned about where his little monkey has been flying.

Wizzie *(from the other side of the stage)*
Can I come over there now or do I have to take out a restrainin' order?

Dorothy
Keep away from me!

Emily *(chiding)*
Dorothy…

Dorothy *(starting to cry, but fighting it tooth and nail)*
Damn it!

(They all cluster around her. Nothing like tears and misery to make folks forget their differences)

Wizzie
Some friend I am. I'm sorry, Dorothy. *(hands her crowbar)* Here, you can whack me if you want. Just don't hit me in the nose. I got two more payments left to go on it yet.

Glinda
I never saw ya cry before.

Dorothy
Yeah. I'm a little rusty at it.

Emily
When I was small and fell into melancholy, my mother would always bring me a treat. Something warm—

(A hunky young lad starts walking past downstage)

Glinda *(watching him)*
—And sweet.

(She whispers to Wizzie, who whispers to Emily, who nods and approaches the stud muffin; she talks quickly and quietly to him, gesturing toward Dorothy)

Dorothy *(almost in a trance)*
'Melancholy'…sounds like a dog that eats cantaloupe.

Glinda
Huh?

Dorothy
'Cantaloupe'…sounds like what Juliet shoulda said to Romeo.

Glinda
You OK?

Dorothy *(wakes herself out of her funk)*
Say what? Oh…I'll live, I guess. More than I can say for Frank.

Wizzie
Aw, he's a creep. Forget him.

Dorothy
Couldn't you have had that blazin' realization about eight years ago? Woulda saved us all this trouble.

Wizzie
Oh, I always knew he was a creep. I'm just a slut. *(pause)* Hey, that's where yer all s'posed to jump up and say, "No, no, Wizzie, yer not a slut. Yer just lonely and misunderstood."

Dorothy/Glinda *(robotically, barely keeping a straight face)*
"No, no, Wizzie, yer not a slut. Yer just lonely and misunderstood."

Wizzie
Damn right.

Emily *(bringing the young man up to the group)*
Dorothy, I'd like to introduce someone to you. This is Gale.

Gale
Hi.

Wizzie *(steps forward)*
Hi!

Glinda *(yanking her back)*
Misunderstood, my ass.

Dorothy *(adjusting her hair and clothes)*
Hi, there. Nice tattoo. What is that?

Gale *(flexes bicep)*
A rainbow.

Dorothy
Really? I adore rainbows. *(Emily hands her something)* What's this?

Emily *(whispering)*
Key to the trailer, dear. Kindly replace any pictures that get knocked off the walls.

Dorothy *(smiles)*
Yes'm. *(starts walking up right with Gale, arm-in-arm)*

Emily
Back to work, ladies.

(Emily, Wizzie, and Glinda scatter about the stage, in the positions they were in before the fight. Dorothy is still walking with Gale)

Dorothy *(stroking his butt)*
You know, when I was club dancing I used to have a move I called The Rainbow.

Gale
Really?

Dorothy
Used to triple my tips. Maybe I'll show it to you.

(They are off up right as the lights fade out)

STRUMPET VOLUNTARY

A play by Terry Kroenung
© 2002

SCENE: *A garden of one of Louis XIV's palaces, 1690's. A dance is in progress through the doors off left. Its music can be faintly heard.*

SET: *Double doors SL; marble benches DL and DR; gazebo with vines and flowers UC; a Corinthian pillar topped with a Cupid on either side of it.*

AURORE, late teens, very lovely and innocent-looking, bursts in through the SL doors. The music gets louder as the doors are opened. She wears a stunning dress and a wicked grin. Fanning herself furiously, she steps to the gazebo, snips a flower from it with scissors from her bodice, then goes to the UR pillar and hides.

LA MAUPIN enters a moment later through the same doors. She closes them quickly and leans against them, peering about the garden. She is in her mid-twenties. Dressed as a man, complete with wig and sword, her disguise should be believable to a naïve girl. She holds Aurore's handkerchief.

She frowns, then smiles and moves to the gazebo stealthily. Leaping into it, she finds nothing. Aurore peeks around her pillar. La Maupin tiptoes toward the UR pillar. Aurore slips around it on the SL side and enters the gazebo unseen. La Maupin rushes at the UR pillar, again finds nothing. Aurore giggles, stifles it, gets out of sight in the gazebo's foliage. La

Maupin smiles at this, goes to the SL doors, opens one, slams it, then rushes to hide herself behind the UL pillar. Aurore laughs, rushes out from the gazebo to LC. La Maupin moves in behind her, wraps an arm around her waist, kisses her neck.

La Maupin
Once more the swan falls prey to the fox.

Aurore *(sigh)*
Ohhh, Monsieur…has the advantage of me.

La Maupin
I sincerely hope so. *(spins her around for a long kiss)*

Aurore
What would the nuns at my school say if they could see me now?

La Maupin
They would probably say, "Hurry up and finish with him so we can have our turn!"

Aurore *(playfully whacking her with the fan)*
Sir, you are wicked!

La Maupin
You have no idea.

Aurore *(steps away SR)*
Oh, I think I do. I saw you dance with a dozen ladies in there, including the King's Wednesday mistress, Madame Ehonte. Your hands were roaming like gypsies over the countryside.

La Maupin
Well, she has a lovely…countryside. Alas, gypsies are never welcome in new lands for long. *(advances on her)* They tend to steal away with precious treasure…boldly taken in the night.

Aurore *(backing away DR)*
What if the strongbox is well-guarded?

La Maupin *(still advancing)*
Locks, bars, dogs, walls...they "are no stop to me."

Aurore *(still backing DR)*
"For stony limits cannot hold love out."

La Maupin
So it has been said.

Aurore *(backing into and sitting on DR bench)*
It must be true. We are inside the lovely walls already. *(indicates garden)*

La Maupin *(smirk)*
Not quite yet. *(sitting beside her)* Perhaps later.

Aurore *(closing her eyes, leaning her head back)*
Ohhh...

La Maupin *(stroking her neck, trailing a finger down her throat)*
My fair young swan. Such delicate beauty that has known no rough touch of hunter, nor terror of cage or pen.

Aurore
Not true. The nuns—

La Maupin *(touching her hair)*
—Are not here. Sssh...let me preen your plumage, my trembling little cygnet.

Aurore
Your touch enchants. Your voice enthralls. Do it again. Please.

La Maupin
Do what?

Aurore

Weave a spell with your voice again. Sing to me, sir, just like you sang to all of us in there only an hour ago. I can still feel your silken notes caressing my soul like the falling petals of a weeping flower.

La Maupin

You would hear that same song? The English one?

Aurore

I would listen to it again and again…until the moon goes dark and the sun deserts the heavens.

La Maupin

Mayhap you would be surfeited before then.

Aurore

Impossible. Does the bee sicken on the nectar it sucks from the blossom?

La Maupin *(kissing her tenderly)*

We may have an answer by the morning. *(standing)* I must accede to my lady's gentle request.

(singing John Dowland's "Come again: sweet love it now doth invite")

Come again:
Sweet love doth now invite,
Thy graces that refrain,
To do me such delight,
To see, to hear, to touch, to kiss, to die
With thee again in sweetest sympathy.

Come again
That I may cease to mourn,
Through thy unkind disdain:
For now left and forlorn,
I sit, I sigh, I weep, I faint, I die

In deadly pain and endless misery.
Gentle Love,
Draw forth thy wounding dart,
Thou canst not pierce her heart,
For I that to approve,
By sighs and tears more hot than are thy shafts,
Did tempt while she for triumph laughs.

(ends song standing behind Aurore)

Aurore *(sighing)*
    Oh, I dare not laugh at you, monsieur.

La Maupin *(stroking her neck)*
    Why not? Venus does, with every plunge of her sightless son's shaft into a helpless male bosom.

Aurore
    You, helpless? *(laughing)*

La Maupin
    Ah! You see?

Aurore *(jumping up)*
    No! "I rather weep…at thy good heart's oppression."

La Maupin
    Your convent school teaches Shakespeare well. But I would not be the cause of a single wretched tear blemishing that flawless face. Not even for love's pity.

Aurore *(moving toward DC)*
    My pity is not for your pangs of desire, sir.

La Maupin
    No?

Aurore
Rather my sorrow is at your lack of worthy prey.

La Maupin
You misprize yourself, Lady Aurore.

Aurore
I think not. I saw in there *(indicates SL doors)* how you moved through the hall...as Alexander surveying his dominions. Not a woman breathed your essence without falling under the effortless spell of Eros.

La Maupin *(smiles)*
Now you overprize me.

Aurore
Do I? How many different ladies did you kiss tonight? How many different hands were held? How many strategically-dropped lace handkerchiefs did you return to their blushing and ever-so-grateful owners?

La Maupin
It would not be gallant to keep count.

Aurore
And all without the slightest exertion on your part. Gliding from one conquest to the other with an aura of inevitability.

La Maupin
Please, you'll turn my head.

Aurore
That would be the greatest strain I have seen from you all evening. You swept through us like a sweet pestilence—no hope of cure or resistance. Are you even aware of it?

La Maupin
No more than **you** were of your effect on that gilded cage of pea-cocks, strutting and preening for your approval.

Aurore (*DL now*)
Now you mock me, sir.

La Maupin (*crossing to her*)
I swear I do not. They were tripping over their flowered pumps to attract your attention.

Aurore
To whom can you be referring?

La Maupin
To that trio of young fops whose self-worth was being held cap-tive by your ineffable radiance. They might have been lapdogs leashed on a bejeweled chain, no farther did they ever move from you.

Aurore
Oh, they were merely showing courtesy to a lonely guest.

La Maupin
Then they were most discourteous to every other lady in the room.

Aurore (*hiding behind her fan*)
Every other lady was on **your** leash, monsieur.

La Maupin (*lowering her fan with a finger*)
Mongrels, all. I saw only one purebred.

Aurore
Ohh…

La Maupin
Unsullied of pedigree. Unstained in demeanor.

Aurore
Ah, monsieur…

La Maupin
Standing out from that yelping pack of bitches as does a serene swan amidst a flock of shrieking ravens. *(moves behind her)* My lovely Aurore, daughter of the dawn…

Aurore
All those dances. All those handkerchiefs.

La Maupin
Ask not how many I returned. *(caresses her with the handkerchief she brought in at the beginning)* Ask how many I kept. *(breathes in the handkerchief's scent)* Sweet as a sinner's repentance.

(she kisses Aurore's neck; one hand wraps around her waist; the other glides across her bosom)

Aurore *(lost to rational thought; a sigh)*
Sweet mother Mary…

(Aurore drops a hand behind and between them, obviously to grope La Maupin's "nether regions"; she freezes and shrieks)

Aurore
Sweet mother Mary! *(jerks away, moves across the bench)*

La Maupin *(philosophical)*
Ah, well…'twas bound to come out.

Aurore
Come out? Taken out!

La Maupin
I beg your pardon?

Aurore *(pointing)*
Your—Your—!

La Maupin
Undercarriage? Yes, well...

Aurore
You poor man...how did it happen?

La Maupin *(realizing that she has not been discovered)*
Oh...it is a tale hardly fit for your hearing. Not part of the nuns' curriculum, I would venture to say.

Aurore *(sitting on DL bench)*
Please. If your sensibilities can withstand it.

La Maupin *(warming to the story she is hastily inventing)*
I am not a nobleman. My parents were poor farmers. As their only son, I was their treasure. And the hope of their old age, of course. My mother spoiled me terribly. No request of mine was too extreme to be granted. I fear I abused her sweetness terribly. It shames me now to think on it. My father was a simple solid man. No one ever worked harder to give his little family a good life.

We were unpretentious, God-fearing people. Other than the unremitting backbreaking toil which filled our days—and many of our nights as well—all we had was our faith. Every Sunday we were on our knees in the parish church, hearing Mass from old Father Girarde. And every Sunday, too, I would sing for the worshippers. I can well recall, even as young as seven or eight, singing the praises of God in that tiny village church.

<u>Aurore</u>

With a voice given to you by that same God.

<u>La Maupin</u>

By God? No, by Satan! For it could only have been the machinations of the Lord of the Infernal Regions that stole me from my sainted parents' side one black night in my eleventh year.

To this day I do not know who saw me in that little church, which of my trusted fellow townsmen heard me sing and devised a devilish plan to profit from my misery. But one dark December night saw a foul-smelling sack thrown over my head as I came out of the privy. I could scarcely breathe. Next I knew I was being hurled onto the bed of a wagon and trussed up like a pig bound for slaughter. Little did I know how apt that description was!

After hours of suffering I was tossed into an unlit room, still tied fast. For what seemed like days I lay there in terror, crying for someone—anyone—to come to my aid. What must my parents have been thinking, when I seemed to disappear from the face of the earth? I prayed to the God I had so often sung to, to deliver me from this evil. When at last the door opened, and food and water were given me, I believed my pitiful pleas had finally been heard. Such was my naivete.

A harsh voice whispered in my ear, "You are blessed with a mighty instrument, young master. Rare it is that heaven bestows such a gift. And we are here to see that it remains with you always." With that my breeches were rudely pulled down. I struggled with desperate strength but I was held fast by four men with sinews of iron. Something cold and wet was poured on my…my nether regions. I smelled brandy. An instant later I felt an agony sharp and shrill that few in this blessed world are cursed to endure. How I sang then! My throat sent a note to Heaven such as it had never produced before. But all I heard in reply, before I mercifully fainted, was a holy echo.

I awoke who knows how many days later…fevered, delirious. A strange woman nursed me. She, at least, was kind. It was she who, gently as she could, broke the news to me that my budding manhood had been cruelly cut from me, in order that my sweet voice would always endure. It was she who held me as I sobbed for what had been lost and could never be regained. It was she who cured me of my infection and allowed me to live.

When I was able to leave my bed she turned me over to a pair of well-dressed men who taught me to sing...or suffer. I was beaten when I resisted, I was beaten when I missed a note, was beaten when I cried from being beaten. But I was lodged like a lord, clothed like a prince, and fed like a king. Yet always I remained a captive songbird, despite the gaudy ornaments on the cage.

I soon discovered that my jailers were opera impresarios, and I was their ticket to further fortune. After several attempted escapes they introduced me to Guido, a deaf-mute Italian with a sharp knife and even sharper nose for my childish plans. It was made clear to me that there were even more valuable assets remaining to be severed from my young body, should I persist on seeking my freedom. When I manfully declared that I cared nothing for my useless life, that God would receive me with open arms, they sneered that I surely cared for the life of my mother, which would be brutally snuffed out if I should ever run away again.

I was beaten. If they could find me to kidnap me, they could certainly find my mother to harm her. I acquiesced to their every demand, resigned to be their canary. Once I proved that I was theirs, they became the soul of generosity. As long as I sang, my every whim was indulged. I had the best tutors, tailors, and wigmakers in Paris. I learned to command every skill a gentleman was expected to master: riding, shooting, dancing, fencing. My masters introduced me to great courtiers, to greats of the Opera, to great men and women in all walks of life. Though not noble, I quickly mastered the art of seeming to be so...which is more than half the battle.

So you see before you a man, at least in every way but one, who has achieved—through untold suffering—all that any man could desire...save the love of a pure woman. The love of a virtuous woman who cares more for my soul than the contents of my breeches.

(sits beside Aurore) Are you she, Lady Aurore? Are you the Heloise who will save this Abelard?

Aurore *(in tears)*
  Oh, monsieur…!

(Applause from DR and DL, offstage. From each corner a ridiculously well-dressed young man enters, looking very similar to La Maupin, actually. The DL gentleman is Chevalier **TEMERAIRE** *and the DR gentleman is the Vicomte du* **VILEPENDER**. *Each is armed)*

Vilepender *(moving to DRC)*
  Bravo! Your finest performance! I was enchanted! *(to Temeraire)* Weren't you enchanted, Jaques?

Temeraire *(stopping behind Aurore)*
  Indubitably.

Vilepender
  I'm of a mind to write a review for one of those broadsheets one sees posted about town. "Last night at the sumptuous ball given by the Duc du Orleans, attended by the Sun King himself, a stirring—one might almost say moving performance—was given by a performer whose previous work was as nothing compared to what this noble audience enjoyed." *(to La Maupin)* By the way, was there the slightest germ of truth in that heart-rending speech you just gave to this beautiful but admittedly naïve young faun?

La Maupin
  Well…I did have a mother.

Temeraire
  Doing penance in hell for the deed, I daresay.

La Maupin *(eyeing him cooly)*
You, Chevalier, will be the first tonight to go there…to see if you are correct.

Temeraire *(snorts)*
'Twill take more than bitch singer to accomplish that.

Vilepender
My apologies for Temeraire's manners. He's always forgetful of courtly niceties when he is spurned; however, he does have a point.

La Maupin *(fingering her sword hilt)*
So do I. Where would you like to feel it, Vicomte? Your belly or your throat?

Vilepender
Such fire! Such passion in the face of adversity. I do believe you almost deserve the plaudits you gain at the Opera.

Aurore
Gentlemen, can we not go back inside? I am certain I owe dances to you both.

Temeraire
You owe us a good deal more than that. And you'll pay up. *(touches her chin)* Oh, how you'll pay.

La Maupin *(her sword is instantly out and at his breast)*
She owes you nothing. But I do.

Vilepender *(waving Temeraire back)*
Time enough for that later, Jacques. Anything worth doing is worth doing well.

La Maupin
At last we are in agreement on something, Vilepender.

Aurore
My lords, please…this gentleman has done you no harm.

Temeraire

Gentleman?! *(laughs)*

Vilepender

I am afraid, Lady Aurore, that you have been the victim of a cruel deception. That is why we are here. So that the truth may breathe freely.

La Maupin

That won't happen until you and your kind let go of its throat. Aurore, go. Quickly.

Aurore

I want to stay here with you and—

La Maupin

Now!

*(Aurore bolts for the door. Temeraire tries to stop her, but is cut off by La Maupin. Aurore flings open a door, and runs into another young gentleman, the Chevalier de **CHATRER**. He holds her firmly and brings her back into the garden, stopping to close the door. He remains between it and La Maupin. He, too, is armed)*

Vilepender

It pays to take precautions. Now that my good friend Chatrer is arrived, our little party can begin. Where was I? Ah! Yes, my lady, you have been deceived. This is no gentleman.

Aurore *(shrugging free of Chatrer, who releases her but guards her)*

It is true he is of humble birth, he has admitted as much to me; however, his nobility of manner has had no peer in my experience.

(All three young men are laughing heartily at this)

Vilepender
Those nuns really should let you out more often, my dear. You need more experience.

Chatrer
We aren't talking about his 'manner'.

Temeraire
We're talking about his empty breeches.

Aurore
I see no need to taunt the poor man just because he was cruelly used.

Chatrer
"Poor man"!

Temeraire
Lost them in the war, did he?

Vilepender
The only poor man who has been cruelly used here this evening has been myself…and my two handsome friends, of course.

Chatrer
Because we're the only poor men here.

Temeraire
Because we're the only **men** here at all!

Aurore
I don't under—

Vilepender *(to La Maupin)*
For God's sake, tell her, will you? I'll wager she'd have found out later tonight anyway if we hadn't come along.

Aurore *(looking at La Maupin)*
Monsieur?

La Maupin
Not quite. *(removes her man's wig to reveal her red-blonde hair)* My name is Julie D'Aubigny. Better known at the Opera as La Maupin. I apologize for selling you fraudulent merchandise. *(takes Aurore's hand, places it on her bosom)* But I declare that my heart is true, my lady. *(kisses her tenderly; then she whispers something to her that neither the men nor audience can here)* You understand me?

(Aurore nods. She appears stunned and frightened. She looks around the garden as if looking for a rock to hide under)

La Maupin
All this, then, is for your wounded male pride? Because she preferred me to you louts?

Temeraire
Louts? That's a gentlemanly word.

Chatrer
Such nobility of manner.

Temeraire
Like a beautiful aria.

Chatrer
Or a hymn.

Temeraire
A would-be 'him', anyway.

Chatrer
Or a 'strumpet voluntary'!

Temeraire
Oh, that's a good one!

La Maupin
I am sorry, my lords. I meant to say "you pricks".

Vilepender *(laughs)*
I'll say this for you, Mademoiselle La Maupin…I shall miss your wit.

La Maupin
Why? Am I going somewhere?

Vilepender *(drawing his sword)*
Oh, I rather think so.

Chatrer *(drawing his sword)*
The bottom of the Seine, most likely.

Temeraire *(drawing his sword)*
Or maybe just a cesspool someplace.

Vilepender
But I can promise you that we'll take up a collection to have your friends at the Opera sing a requiem mass for you. A last goodbye for one of their own.

La Maupin
Save your money for your own funerals. Worry not, I'll sing there for free. Now, Aurore!

(La Maupin reaches into Aurore's décolletage and pulls out her bodice scissors. Aurore stamps on Chatrer's foot. He winces and catches her fan in his face. This enables her to get behind La Maupin and into the gazebo.
La Maupin fights with the scissors closed as a parrying dagger. All three men attack her. She dispatches Temeraire first, as she had promised, at ULC. The other two become more cautious. The fight moves over the

whole stage. Chatrer falls DR, leaving only Vilepender. He is elegant with a sword, as is La Maupin. They are a joy to watch. She wounds him seriously but not mortally. He falls DC. Aurore rushes up to embrace La Maupin)

Aurore
I was so frightened for you!

La Maupin *(kisses her cheek)*
You should have been more frightened **of** me, my swan. *(to Vilepender; touching his face gently)* I give you the same belated advice, my lord.

Vilepender
I thought three of us would serve.

La Maupin *(smiling, looking from him to Aurore)*
Perhaps so. *(helps him to his feet)* We can attend to you at my apartment.

Aurore
We?

La Maupin
Of course. And we should hurry before the Duc's guards wonder what been going on out here.

Aurore *(very confused)*
Just what **has** been going on out here?

La Maupin *(taking her hand and kissing it)*
Life. *(kisses Vilepender)* Life. Write to the nuns that you've found a better school. Please make sure that you spell my name correctly.

(Lights fade as they help Vilepender out DR; all exit)

WEST

A play by Terry Kroenung
© 2003

SCENE: *Assistant commandant's office, German concentration camp; spring, 1945.*

SET: *Door SL and in UR corner (in SR wall). Desk SR, facing DL. Besides the usual office items, it also has a liquor bottle on it. Comfortable executive chair behind desk. Armless chair facing it. Metal cabinet UC. Floor lamp SR of cabinet. Coat rack at SL door. Imagined window DC.*

KLAUS BEDAUERN, late 30's, the acting camp commander, stands DC, looking out of the "window". He smokes a cigarette, which is nearly finished, and toys with his SS dagger. He is in full uniform, collar undone, but his holster is empty. His mistress, CHRISTINE, late 20's, sits on the desk in a white slip, red high heels, and his cap. She is playing with his pistol, "shooting" imagined enemies with appropriately childish sound effects. She is coming off a recreational morphine dose.

Artillery can be heard in the distance. It will be heard throughout the play, becoming progressively louder. Occasionally a plane or two flies past and trucks roll by outside the window.

The floor lamp is on. It is very late at night.

Klaus
Thirty kilometers.

Christine
Hmm?

Klaus
Sounds like they're about thirty kilometers east of us. They'll be here in a day or two, at the rate they've been moving.

Christine
The Americans?

Klaus
East!

Christine
Not the Americans?

Klaus
Soviets. *(under his breath)* Dimwit.

Christine
Oh, the Russians. It must be true. They're certainly "rushin'" to get here. *(laughs hysterically)*

Klaus *(rolls his eyes; mutters)*
My mistake. **Half**wit.

Christine *("shooting" him in the back)*
You know, the morphine doesn't make me deaf.

Klaus
Nor any smarter.

Christine

Look who's talking. The Commandant abandons us here for Uruguay and you raise your hand like a good little Nazi: "Gee, I'd love to be in charge of this camp when the Russians break down the gate. What an honor!"

Klaus

Pinhead.

Christine (*goes to him, hugs him from behind, strokes his chest*)

You should try to be nice to people.

Klaus (*wry laugh*)

It's a tad late in the day for that, don't you think? Am I supposed to start adding good deeds to my side of the balance now, to tip the scales of eternal justice against the outraged shades of a couple of million butchered Jews?

Christine (*gives him a playful swat*)

I said you should be nice to **people**, silly. Pay attention to me, will you?

Klaus (*softly*)

Late in the day for that, too.

(*knock on SL door*)

Klaus

Enter!

(*A camp **INMATE**, a woman, enters, bows*)

Woman

Commandant, they have found the one you asked for.

Klaus
 When?

Woman
 This morning, in the train from Zagreb.

Klaus
 Was she treated as I directed?

Woman
 Your orders were followed perfectly.

Klaus
 Good. Have her brought here.

Woman
 At once. *(bows, exits)*

Christine
 "Her"? Should I go and change the sheets?

Klaus
 Shut up.

Christine
 Late in the day for that, too. *(returns to desk, sits on it again; lays pistol aside)* Who's this one? Another clear-skinned Gypsy teenager? You sure you can keep "up" with her after all the schnapps you've guzzled today?

Klaus
 You're one to talk, after working your way through my enlisted men.

Christine
 Oh, I'm sorry. Are you telling me to keep my hands off your privates? *(giggles)*

Klaus

And save some morphine for the wounded, why don't you?

Christine

What wounded? They don't stop running long enough to get shot. A few sprained ankles, maybe. Pretty soon the inmates will be guarding themselves. *(crosses to him, takes his cigarette, puts it in her mouth)* So, who is she?

Klaus

No one. Just another Jew with a chimney appointment.

Christine

Except that this one also has an appointment with the camp commandant. Why might that be, I have to wonder?

Klaus

Wonder till you turn blue. It's camp business.

Christine

And here I thought I'd been **getting** the camp business all this time.

Klaus

Shut up. Go to your room and sleep it off. *(pause)* I'll...be there later.

Christine *(licks her lips)*

You bringing her with you?

Klaus

Why? It's not your birthday.

Christine

As if you have a clue when that is.

Klaus

That's because I suspect you don't have one. More likely you came out of Mengele's lab.

Christine *(whispering in his ear)*
    Built to your exacting specifications. *(exits UR; takes pistol from desk as she goes)*

Klaus *(to himself)*
    Then I should have been more specific…*(aloud, at her back)* I left you a card on the night table.

(He goes behind the desk, buttoning his collar. He checks to ensure his uniform is perfect as a knock is heard at the SL door. He straightens the desk, puts liquor bottle in UC cabinet. Another knock. He makes a final survey of the room, scabbards his dagger, buttons the holster.)

Klaus
    Come in.

*(The Woman enters with **JUDITH FRIEDHOF**, who is still in the filthy clothes she arrived in: trousers, man's shirt, boots. She has been given an army greatcoat, however. Her hair has not been cut. In her late 20's, she is striking but not beautiful.)*

Woman
    The Friedhof woman, Herr Commandant.

Klaus
    Good. Dismissed.

(She nods and exits SL. Judith stands at C. Klaus moves to stand directly in front of her)

Klaus *(after a pause)*
    Fraulein.

Judith
Major Bedauern.

Klaus (*after a pause*)
Seat?

Judith
No. I've been sitting on the floor of a cattle car for four days.

Klaus (*reaching for her face*)
My poor Judith—

Judith (*jerking her head away*)
Don't.

Klaus (*crosses toward desk*)
Ah…so I'm to pretend that we are merely jailer and inmate, then?

Judith
Pretend? I've been locked up with the dead and dying for the better part of a week, up to my ass in their puke and shit, nearly deaf from their pathetic pleadings to an indifferent God. Five miles away from here we started gagging from the chimney stench. Inside the gate we were herded between head-high heaps of contorted corpses while the guards cackled like lunatics. My entire group, those not pulled lifeless from the car onto the frozen ground, were shoved shrieking into your so-called showers. At the last second I was yanked aside and dragged to a barracks. Now I'm here. Precisely where is the pretense, Herr Jailer?

Klaus (*after a pause*)
At least take off your coat.

Judith
Why, does some shivering soldier need it back?

Klaus *(smashing a hand on the desk)*
God damn you!

Judith
Truer words were never spoken.

(Removes her coat, throws it at him. He catches it, folds it carefully, places it atop the cabinet)

Judith
Somehow that reminds me of a mortician carefully preparing the body.

Klaus
There was a time when you didn't particularly mind my preparing your body.

Judith
That stupid girl died years ago. I buried her under ten tons of remorse. You can't send her up your chimney. *(pause)* What's going on here?

Klaus
It's complicated.

Judith
You thought I'd walk in here and throw myself breathlessly into your manly arms? "Oh, Klaus, you saved me from the gas! Take me, my love!"

Klaus
Not at all.

Judith
Because I have to tell you, moonlight and candles on the Rhine this isn't.

Klaus
Stop...

Judith
Granted, there is a certain ineffable charm to the warm glow of the crematory fires. And the piles of glasses and dentures make for an erotic ambience a girl would be hard put to resist.

Klaus (*moving toward her*)
Please...You don't—

Judith
I have to confess that the dead bodies of the desperate tangled in the electric fence **do** make me think of romance, somehow.

Klaus
Judith—

Judith
They remind me of how I'd like to cut your heart out, just like you did mine when you started butchering my people wholesale!

Klaus (*slapping her*)
Shut up!

(*pause*)

Judith (*doesn't move*)
Yes, that's the sentimental lover I remember. If memory serves, that was your parting kiss in '39. The taste of blood really takes me back to the good old days.

Klaus
Don't try to put it all on me.

Judith

Not at all. I place all the blame on me. If I hadn't been such a naïve, starry-eyed child to think I could make a decent human being of you, we would never have ended up in the same bed.

Klaus *(wryly)*

Many a good man has been created in those circumstances.

Judith

Every good man…and every bad one, too. *(wavers, grabs back of armless chair)*

Klaus *(grabbing her arm and putting her in the chair)*

Come on, sit. No arguing.

(She sits, leans over to forestall fainting)

Klaus

This comes of trying to be a superwoman, running around Yugoslavia blowing up our trains.

Judith

So surrender, if you care so much for my welfare.

Klaus *(very softly)*

That happened long ago. *(pause)* Didn't they feed you when you arrived? I left orders.

Judith

Potato soup, a little beef, some black bread. But six years living on slogans and honor can't be countered in a day.

Klaus *(opening UC cabinet)*

I'll have more sent in. *(pours her a drink from the bottle he had placed there)* Here.

Judith (*takes it reluctantly, sniffs at it*)
Ah...you were drinking this when we met.

Klaus
I've drunk nothing else since.

Judith
Who would guess that the master of...(*indicates camp*) all this...would be so sentimental?

Klaus
That's your doing.

Judith
The sentiment, or all this?

Klaus
That's a foolish question.

Judith
No. 'Why would a good Jewish girl fall in love with an SS officer?. **That's** a foolish question.

Klaus
Please don't say it was the uniform.

Judith
I think it looks pretty silly, truth be told.

Klaus
As do I, actually. Should I take it off?

Judith
Far too late for that. You should never have put it on.

Klaus
Agreed.

Judith
Is that an epiphany I smell?

Klaus
Something like that.

Judith (*sniffs*)
Strange…it smells like cheap perfume. Does she know about me?

Klaus
No.

Judith
Ashamed of your old Jewish mistress?

Klaus
Ashamed, yes…but never of you.

Judith
And here I was dreaming of that touching bedroom scene where you roll over, light her cigarette, and say, "Darling, did I ever tell you about my lover, the rabbi's daughter? We met in moonlight…"

Klaus (*quietly, at the window, more to himself than to her*)
"…moonlight. It caught in her black hair like stars in a net. Her blue dress caressed her long luscious legs as she danced with old Colonel Haupt. Some of us wished we were him. I wished I was the dress. Every man in the room knew she was a Jew, and probably a spy, and none gave a damn. They moved on her as if she were a fortress to be taken by storm, and their battalions broke upon her defenses. I could see she would never fall to a blitzkrieg, only to a gentle siege."

Judith (*snorts*)
Gentle!

Klaus

"All the time I was cocooning her in music and tenderness, I believed that I was undermining her bastion. Imagine my surprise when I reached for my heart one summer night and found it in her iron grasp."

Judith

Would you like it back?

Klaus

An exchange of prisoners? Against current Wehrmacht regulations, I'm afraid. *(pause)* "That September she fled the field, to wage war anew in other killing grounds. I pursued, but she melted into the fog of battle. Vague intelligence reports hinted at her movements: assassinations in Warsaw, kidnappings in Bucharest, prisoner rescues in Prague. Always a Dark Angel was mentioned, the last lovely lethal memory of our men. And then her phenomenal luck finally broke in Zagreb. She fell into our eager hands like a delightful surprise gift, all unlooked for. Naturally she was sent to me, for...final processing." And a last reckoning.

Judith

You always did tell a good story. "I know no touch of it, my lord".

Klaus *(smiles)*

"'Tis as easy as lying."

Judith

Just because you wear black it doesn't make you Hamlet.

Klaus

Well, I do have relatives in Denmark.

Judith

So did I. *(glares at him)* But they're all dead now. They were last seen at your cozy train station. *(pause)* Shall we jump ahead to the fifth act, since we've seen this play before? The stage is already set for it—bodies everywhere, enemy army at the gates, characters choking on their own guilt...

Klaus *(to himself)*
Flawed hero about to be redeemed through sacrifice and death.

Judith *(not hearing)*
So let's ring down the curtain on this tragic farce, hm? Thank you for the last meal, and the last drink. But we both know how the show ends. Let's get going.

Klaus
What?

Judith
Give me a bar of soap and point me toward the showers. I'm eager to wash off the muck of this miserable world.

Klaus
You...? No! *(goes to her)* Judith, love, you're reading from the wrong script.

Judith
No, no. It says right here: "We owe God a death."

Klaus
He's been overpaid already. You have a refund coming.

Judith *(suspicious now)*
What are you talking about?

Klaus
This isn't **Hamlet**. The heroine lives. *(draws his dagger, places it in her hands)* It is the tragic hero only who must fall.

Judith *(stepping back)*
Oh! You miserable Christians! You set fire to the entire blessed world and then think you can atone for the conflagration by falling on a knife?

Klaus

No. I just want out of a burning building.

Judith

Then what—? *(finally gets it)* Ah…then this is *Julius Caesar*.

Klaus *(nods)*

Only without the honor.

Judith *(holds the dagger out to him)*

Find yourself another Strato, Brutus.

Klaus

Too late. You auditioned for the role six years ago.

Judith

No! I walked out on the production.

Klaus

It's not that easy!

Judith

I will **not** do this!

Klaus

Why not? You had no trouble cutting the throats of those five Gestapo men in Bucharest.

Judith

They weren't running up to me, eager to taste the blade. It was combat.

Klaus

So is this, my little commando! Look around you! This is how wars end! The losers bleed out their little lives in bathrooms or courtrooms and the rest of you march off to write smug history books.

Judith *(buries the dagger blade in the armless chair)*
Write it yourself! My inkwell is dry.

Klaus
You need motivation, then? A superobjective? *(goes to desk, takes another knife from a drawer)* How about survival? Hot blood instead of cold?

Judith
And I thought the situation was as surreal as it could get.

Klaus *(walking toward her)*
I will **not** be a rag doll dancing on Russian bayonets.

Judith
And I will not make this easy for you! If you want to open your veins to cheat them, then do it! Don't cry to me to help you along.

Klaus
No crying, no begging. If it's the shock of combat you need…*(slashes at her, misses)*

Judith *(jumping back, away from the chair and the dagger)*
Are you out of your mind?

Klaus
Not any more. I had a six-year mad scene, but it just ended. *(thrusts; she evades it)* Come on, Dark Angel! Miss Freedom Fighter! *(gets between her and the SL door)* Earn your liberty.

Judith
And get shot two steps out that door.

Klaus
I gave the guards written orders to let you go. There's a car behind this building. Take the road west. I left a signed pass on the seat. Go west and get into the American lines.

(He cuts at her. She controls his wrist, pulls him past, and makes for the door. He catches her from behind by the hair, hurls her at the chair where her dagger waits. He thrusts. She parries with the chair, still unwilling to use the dagger)

Judith

This is lunacy!

Klaus

And just how are we judging madness these days? Is this crazier than filling pits full of sobbing, writhing civilians? Than enslaving tiny children? Than boiling your family for soap?

(She wails, pulls the knife from the chair, attacks him. He parries)

Klaus

Ah, finally some heat. You'll have to try harder. I won't just stand still for you. You see, this isn't so much *Julius Caesar* as it is *Macbeth*...lay on, Jew bitch!

(The fight intensifies. She presses him SL, toward the door. He knocks her back with the coat rack)

Klaus

Pretty good for a Christ-killing harpie! Let's go! You only get out this door over my dead body! Don't pretend that distresses you.

(Fight intensifies again. They use the whole room)

Klaus

I hunted your people with a religious fervor when you left. Like I was on a mission from God. Shot cripples in the head, buried babies alive, burned expectant mothers naked and shrieking in their miserable synagogues!

(Fight goes into a frenzy, ending in a taut corps-a-corps at C; Christine enters from UR door with a letter in one hand and the pistol in the other; she watches from there, frozen)

Klaus

Remember…go west. There lies the freedom you've been seeking all this time.

(He lets her envelop his blade upstage. It flies out of his hand. She buries her blade in his chest)

Klaus

I'll be there, waiting for you. *(kisses her, falls)*

(Christine steps into the room, pistol raised. Judith ignores her. She slumps from exhaustion and hunger. Christine moves down behind her, aims the pistol. She wavers as Judith turns to look at her with weary sad eyes. Christine drops the pistol, falls to her knees, still clutching the letter. They embrace, beginning to cry)

(Artillery is heard, very near now. Fade out)

LADIES FIRST

A play by Terry Kroenung
© 2003

<u>SCENE:</u> *A stage combat class under way in a dance studio.*

<u>SET:</u> *Simple open room. Mirrored wall with barre if desired. 2 chairs UC. Entrance DL.*

*(Two pairs of women fight with sword and shield—**MARTHA/DOLLY** and **ABIGAIL/ELEANOR**. They perform the same routine, but not simultaneously. The teacher, **MS. PIERCE**, watches UC, making observations as the fights progress)*

Pierce

Full intention, ladies! Don't let it look too rehearsed...Abigail, watch your targeting...Footwork, footwork!...Martha, good parries tonight...Hey, are we having fun or what?

(The fights wind down at different times. The students relax. Some slump, some drink, some towel off. Martha and Dolly are well apart. Dolly wears arm pads, knee pads, hip pads, etc. Pierce walks DR and dials her cell phone)

Pierce

Hillary? She there yet? Shit! She's cramping my class. You get hold of that snotty two-faced agent of hers and tell her, from me, to have my honored guest down here in five freaking minutes or I'm gonna lose my goddamn professional bearing! *(pockets phone; in lilting "happy" voice)* All right, ladies! How are we doing?

Abigail

Pretty good.

Martha

Sweaty.

Dolly

You're always sweaty.

Martha

Oh, and I suppose that's Dom Perignon all over **your** fat ass?

Eleanor

You want me to taste it and find out?

Dolly

Ugh! You're sick! Stay away from me!

Eleanor

Sheesh! Grow a sense of humor, honey.

Dolly

I have one. It just doesn't recognize you as funny, somehow. *(digging in her bag)* Who wants a Twinkie?

Abigail

Oooo! You know I do.

Martha

I thought George was sharing his Twinkie with you.

Abigail *(handing her a Twinkie)*
I wish. More sponge cake than cream filling there, if you know what I mean.

Eleanor
Typical man.

Dolly
And just how would **you** know?

Eleanor
Hey, I read.

Abigail
Didn't know they had a monosyllabic edition of *Feminist Fight Director.*

Eleanor *(flipping her off with a smile)*
Hey, Abigail, sweetie…can you read this?

Pierce
I hate to break up this Shakespearean exchange, but we do have a class to finish here.

Martha
Sorry. What's next?

Pierce
We still have a couple of minutes till our special guest arrives to run her master class. If you have any questions about your fight…maybe a phrase needs tweaking, or your characterization isn't coming across as you'd like—

Martha *(muttering; glares at Dolly)*
—Or your partner's a backstabbing shit…

Abigail/Eleanor
Ooooo!

Dolly
You gonna harp on that till the Second Coming?

Martha
At least I'll be playing a harp at the Second Coming. There's a special circle of hell for chickies who steal their best friends' parts.

Dolly
Jeez, you act like I slept with the director or something.

Martha
I suspect "or something". Had those knee pads for a while, huh?

Dolly
Hey, Miss Martha, I'm not the one who forgot my underwear at the audition!

Eleanor
What were you doing looking?

Dolly/Martha
Shut up!

Martha
All I know is he told me I had the part, and the next day your name is up there on the call board. What am I supposed to think?

Dolly
Obviously he changed his mind.

Martha
Yeah, after he changed his sheets.

Dolly (*stepping toward her*)
How about I change your nose?

Martha (*squaring off*)
How about I exchange my partner for something loyal, like a dog?

Dolly

Make sure it's a royal bitch, so you can share leashes!

(They jump at one another. Abigail and Eleanor grab and separate them)

Pierce

Ok, Ok. Let's calm down, ladies. Someone wins, someone loses. It's only one audition.

(she takes them aside to mediate, quietly)

Abigail

That's like saying "it's only one lottery", in **this** town.

Eleanor

I don't see what all the fuss is about.

Abigail

That's because the only thing you've ever been cast in was a plumbing commercial.

Eleanor

Hey, don't look down your nose at plumbing! How could your career have gone down the drain without it?

Abigail

My career did not go down a drain!

Eleanor

You're right. My mistake. Technically, a toilet isn't a drain.

Abigail

Pretty strong talk from a girl who grew up in Flushing. Wasn't your drama club called the Queens?

Eleanor
Damn right! When the Flushing Queens took the stage—

Abigail
Took the plunge, you mean—

Eleanor
When the Flushing Queens took the stage, the box office was always backed up.

Abigail
Weren't you guys on public access once?

Eleanor
You bet! We called it "Toilet Pay-Per-View".

Abigail
I would've expected nothing less.

(Pierce brings back the feuding couple)

Pierce
There, now. Isn't this better than scratching each other's eyes out?

Abigail
Best buddies again?

Pierce
Yes. Sometimes stage fighting brings out intense emotions, even in best friends.

Eleanor *(to Martha/Dolly)*
Truce?

Dolly
Yeah, I guess.

Martha

It **was** only one miserable audition.

Dolly

For a part you would've sucked at anyway.

Martha

Look who's talking.

Dolly

That's it! I—

(They have to be separated again. Pierce answers her cell phone DC as Abigail and Eleanor move the feuding pair to opposite corners)

Pierce

Hello? Hillary, I don't want to hear anything out of you except, "She's on her way up the stairs". You don't know what's been going on here. It's like outtakes from *All About Eve*. They—she is?! Woo-hoo! This is the sound of me hugging you through the phone! Thanks, babe! *(hangs up)* Listen up, ladies! Please put the Hatfield-McCoy thing on hold for a while. Our special guest is on her way up. Let's get ready. Gather round.

(The students all move down to her)

Martha

So do we get to know who it is, finally, or do we have to wait till they come through the door?

Eleanor

I can't stand the suspense! I'm about to pee my pants!

Abigail
 Please don't feed me straight lines. I'm only human.

Eleanor
 We're still waiting for the lab results on that one.

Dolly
 Do I have time for a Ho-Ho?

Martha
 Sounds like your director did.

Dolly
 Bite me.

Martha
 Sounds like your director did.

Dolly
 Lay off me!

Martha
 Sounds like your director—

Pierce
 WILL YOU TWO KNOCK IT OFF!

Martha
 Sounds like her—

(Eleanor wraps a towel around Martha's mouth to silence her)

Pierce
 Thank you. All right, I think you should be prepared, to get the maximum benefit out of our guest's visit. You don't know how lucky you are. You are the first class in nearly 25 years to be so fortunate as to get a chance to study with…Desiree du Mont!

Dolly
THE Desiree du Mont?

Eleanor
Star of *The Deadly Skirt*?

Abigail
And *The Musketeers' Mother*?

Dolly
And *Requiem for a Petticoat*?

Pierce
One and the same.

Dolly
Oh, man…I am so turned on!

Martha (*mouth finally free*)
Sounds like your last audition.

Abigail
Give it a rest, why don't you? (*Martha opens her mouth*) You say it and I swear I'll throw you out the window!

Martha
This is all too easy, anyway.

Eleanor
Desiree du Mont! Can you believe it?

Martha
I remember watching her whip up on six guys in *Corsairs in Corsets*. Running up the rigging of the pirate ship, skipping across the yardarm, swinging out on a rope to grab the evil captain in a leg scissors and drop him into the shark-infested sea!

Dolly
   Not remotely her best work. In *Daggers of Desire* she beat a simultaneous attack by the corrupt Marconi triplets with a leap from the balcony straight down into a full split.

Eleanor *(sighing)*
   But it was her elegant whip work in *The Battling Bachelorette* that I'll always remember.

Abigail
   Would you like a cigarette after that fond memory?

Martha
   My fave is the big battle in *Chevalier's Chemise*. When Sterling Holloway and Farley Granger jump her with the poisoned branding irons, she Australian rappels down the side of Canterbury Cathedral with a landsknecht great sword between her teeth, arriving at the burning brothel just in time to dismember Edward Everett Horton and rescue the hooker with the heart of gold.

(They all look at her incredulously)

Eleanor
   I must have missed that one.

Pierce
   Regardless of our tricky memories, I think we can all agree that she is the cinematic feminine beau sabreur par excellance.

Dolly
   Huh?

Abigail *(as to a child)*
   Movie. Babe. Sword fighter. Good.

<u>Dolly</u>
I know **that**!

<u>Martha</u>
I want to ask her about her big affair with Cornell Wilde on the set of *Hell in High Heels.*

<u>Eleanor</u>
Rumored affair.

<u>Martha</u>
Rumored, my Aunt Fanny. Look at the glint in her eye in every corps-a-corps.

<u>Eleanor</u>
Maybe she was looking at the script girl over his shoulder.

<u>Abigail</u>
You wish.

<u>Pierce</u>
All I know is that this woman made what we do possible.

(Knock on door)

<u>Pierce</u>
Oooh, she's here! Let's greet her in style. Line up over there with your weapons and we'll give her a Ladies First Fight Club salute.

(They do so, forming a line facing the DL entrance)

Pierce
Come in, the door's open! Stand at attention, ladies. I give you the First Lady of the Fight, the Duchess of the Dagger, the Queen of the Quillon! The one, the only, the legendary...Desiree du Mont! Salute! *(they execute a complicated salute)*

(A solitary figure shuffles in. She is 80 if she's a day and looks like Andy Rooney in drag. **DESIREE DU MONT** *uses a walker for locomotion and lugs a small oxygen bottle on her back. She wears a bright pink track suit and sunglasses)*

Desiree *(she has a gravelly voice, like a truck driver after a larynx transplant)*
Hi. How you doin'? Nice salute.

Pierce
Miss Du Mont?

Desiree
Yeah, well, that was just a stage name. You can call me Delores.

Pierce
Delores?

Desiree
Delores Fishbein. Doesn't flow off the tongue like honey, but what the hell. Mom liked it.

Pierce
Well, we're delighted to have you here.

Desiree
Likewise, I'm sure. You got a cigarette? I'm fresh out.

Pierce
Er...no. I'm afraid this is a non-smoking building.

Delores

That bites. This is a wussy town now. Not like in the old days when we had a fifth of bourbon and a pack of Luckies before we were out of the make-up chair. Now it's tofu and bean sprouts, washed down with latte and mineral water. I don't even know what any of that crap is. Oh, well, times change, I guess. Fifty years ago I could break walnuts with my creamy thighs. Now all I can break is wind.

Pierce

Where would you like to start?

Delores

We could have them go through the routine you sent me. I'm pretty familiar with it by now.

Pierce

Alright. Abigail and Eleanor, would you like to go first?

Abigail

Sure. I guess.

(As they get their gear ready, Desiree moves to UC with Pierce, in agonizing slowness. Halfway there she stops to take out a liquor flask and administer herself a large dose. Suitably fortified, she finally makes it to the upstage wall)

Desiree

Go ahead, girls. Knock yourselves out. So to speak.

(Abigail and Eleanor prepare to repeat the fight routine they performed at the beginning of the play, this time with dialogue from one of Desiree's old movies)

<u>Abigail</u>

"At last, Countess la Boom, we meet on the field of honor. I hope, for your sake, that God is not just."

<u>Eleanor</u> *(sneering)*

"Lady Luscious, it will take more than childish taunts to defeat me this time."

<u>Abigail</u>

"Does this look like a child's arm? Behold, it brandishes the sword known as Mabel, Scourge of Evil!"

<u>Eleanor</u>

"Do your worst, little girl!"

(They fight. After the first long phrase, they square off again)

<u>Eleanor</u>

"You fight well, my lady. Someone has been teaching you in secret."

<u>Abigail</u>

"My tutor has been your lover, the handsome but wretched Baron Buttshaft."

<u>Eleanor</u>

"That may be, but you are about to receive your final lesson."

(They fight again. Eleanor falls)

<u>Abigail</u>

"Let that be a lesson to you. Evil can never withstand a righteous blade!"

(Pierce and students applaud. Desiree is asleep and snoring)

Pierce
Miss Du Mont?

Desiree *(jerking awake)*
"Oh, Cornell…let's make this trailer rock!"

Martha *(to Eleanor)*
Told you!

Desiree
All finished? Looked good. Couldn't have done better myself. But there is a little something I could show you.

(She moves with painful slowness to C. She holds out a shaky hand to Abigail)

Desiree
Here, honey, let me see that shield a second.

(Abigail looks nervously to Pierce, who nods. Abigail surrenders the shield)

Desiree *(putting shield on her arm)*
Now, when you use one of these—

(She falls over from the weight of the shield, walker and all. Everyone rushes to help her back up)

Pierce
Are you alright?

Desiree
Oh, yeah. Happens all the time. Guess I should put on some more weight.

Pierce
We can do without the shield demo.

Desiree
Suit yourself. Give me that sword, then. *(Pierce does so)* Nice balance. They make 'em better now than they used to, let me tell ya. In my day you'd finish a fight and your blade would be bent like my first husband's twinkie. *(pause)* Sorry, just reminiscing. Tell you what. One of you be Countess la Boom, and I'll be Lady Luscious.

(Everyone exchanges panicked looks)

Pierce
Are you sure about that?

Desiree
Not a problem. I memorized your fight already.

Pierce
I mean—

Desiree *(waving the sword around indiscriminately, causing all and sundry to duck)*
What?

Pierce
Oh, nothing. I'll be your partner.

(The students heave a collective sigh of relief and rush to the upstage wall. Pierce takes her position)

<u>Desiree</u> *(stopping frequently to gasp for air)*
"At last, Countess...la Boom, we meet on the field of...honor. I hope, for your sake, that"...sorry, honey, only got the one lung now..."God is not just."

<u>Pierce</u> *(gamely, but with much evident concern on her face)*
"Lady Luscious, it will take more than childish taunts to defeat me this time."

<u>Desiree</u> *(holding sword up)*
"Does this look like a child's arm? *(arm falls to her side; she stares at where it had been)* Behold...blah-blah-blah". Gimme a second, will ya, sweetie?" *(She turns up her oxygen canister. There is an immediate change in her)* I thought something wasn't quite right. *(takes a swig from her bottle, tosses it to Abigail)* Let's rock!

(They fight. Desiree moves like a teenager, using the walker as a shield. She is flashy, nimble, thoroughly outclassing Pierce, who ends up on her back, utterly exhausted)

<u>Desiree</u>
Thanks, honey. *(answers her cell phone)* Yeah? Already? Relax, I'm on my way. Pick me up a carton of Luckies while you're at it. And a bottle of Jim Beam. *(hangs up)* Sorry. My agent, Trixie, got her signals crossed. I have to be downtown in twenty minutes for my tae kwan do class. Just send the check to Trixie. You've all been darling. I had a ball. See ya! *(She shuffles out as slowly as she entered, coughing horribly. The students follow her to DL, picking Pierce up off the floor as they go)*

<u>Martha</u>
I always thought she was taller.

(Fadeout)

BOOT CAMP

A play by Terry Kroenung
© 2003

<u>**SCENE**</u>: *A camp for new recruits.*

<u>**SET**</u>: *Open area downstage. Shelves UC, covered by a tarpaulin.*

*(4 recruits sit on the ground at C: <u>**JENNIFER, STEPHANY, JANET**</u>, and <u>**LEE**</u>. All are relatively young. They wear white T-shirts, black military-style fatigue pants, and combat boots. They are exhibiting varying degrees of apprehension)*

<u>Jennifer</u>
It's all this damned waiting that gets to me.

<u>Stephany</u>
Yeah. Let's just get on with it.

<u>Janet</u>
Bring it on! Blow that whistle and get this boot camp going!

<u>Lee</u>
I <u>**can**</u> wait. I'm scared to death.

<u>Stephany</u>
Of what?

<u>Janet</u>
The drill sergeants?

<u>Jennifer</u>
Honey, they're just people like us. Don't start thinking they're side-show freaks or something.

<u>Lee</u>
I've heard stories.

<u>Stephany</u>
Aw, just BS to scare the recruits.

<u>Lee</u>
I don't know. They sounded pretty believable to me.

<u>Janet</u>
Which ones did they tell you? Snake-eating?

<u>Jennifer</u>
Drinking chicken blood?

<u>Stephany</u>
Crawling over hot coals?

<u>Lee</u>
Um...yeah. Pretty much.

<u>Janet</u>
Don't swallow anything those clowns at the reception station feed you.

<u>Jennifer</u>
Bunch of bozos.

Stephany
To hear them tell it, this outfit's a regular 3-ring circus.

Lee
Sounds kinda funny…now that you mention it.

Janet
Course it is. This is the big time. They're all professionals.

Jennifer
No fooling around.

Stephany
They have to prepare us to survive in case the balloon goes up.

Lee
Makes sense.

Janet
Sure it does. They're responsible for our performance. So they won't put up with a lot of silliness.

Lee
That makes me feel better. Thanks, guys!

Stephany
Don't mention it. Where you from, kid?

Lee
Kansas.

Jennifer/Stephany/Janet *(laughing)*
Well, you're not there any more!

Jennifer
Why'd you join up?

Lee
Nothing left at home. No reason to stay.

Janet
No family?

Lee
Mom passed away last year.

Stephany
Rough.

Lee
Yeah. She choked on a...Cracker Jack toy. *(starts to cry)*

Jennifer *(holding her)*
Oh, you poor thing! It's OK. Let it out.

Lee *(sniffing)*
No. I'm here now. I'm going to be tough. This outfit isn't for crybabies.

Janet
Atta girl!

Stephany *(to Janet)*
What about you? Where you from?

Janet
New York. Brooklyn.

Stephany
Yeah? I'm from Jersey myself. Hoboken.

Janet
Got a cousin lives there. You know Vinnie Grimaldi?

Stephany
Hell, yeah! Little guy. Kinda strange. Used to ride a unicycle to school, right through traffic.

Janet
That's him.

Stephany
Went through a box of Band-Aids a week.

Janet
And his mom had 911 on speed dial.

Stephany
Old Vinnie. Small freakin' world. What ever happened to him?

Janet
He's in jail.

Stephany
Sweet little Vinnie Grimaldi's in the joint? What for?

Janet
Caught his wife juggling three boyfriends.

Stephany
Ouch!

Janet
Yeah. So he sawed 'em all in half.

Stephany
I'm telling you...don't piss off those Jersey guys.

Janet
Black and Decker wanted to hire him for a commercial, but the warden wouldn't buy it.

Stephany
Those guys have no sense of humor. *(holds out a hand)* Stephany.

Janet *(shakes)*
Janet.

Stephany *(to Lee)*
Hey, Kansas! You got a name?

Lee
Uh…Lee.

Stephany
Lee, Janet, Stephany…*(to Jennifer)* And your name is—?

Jennifer
Jennifer. California.

Stephany
Cali! So we've got this bi-coastal thing going on here.

Lee
I'm from Kansas.

Stephany
Well, you'll just have to get over that as best as you can.

Janet *(to Jennifer)*
What part of California?

Jennifer *(quietly)*
San Francisco.

Janet/Stephany
Ohhh!

Lee
What's wrong with San Francisco?

Janet
Nothing. Except it's so left-wing the seagulls fly in circles.

Stephany
And the dating scene is a little…unorthodox.

Janet
   Well, boys will be boys…

Janet/Stephany *(laughing)*
   …And so will the girls!

Lee
   I don't get it.

Janet
   You will if you're her bunk mate.

Jennifer
   All right, knock it off. I don't go that way. Understand?

Stephany
   Whatever you say. And what would your story be?

Jennifer
   What do you mean?

Janet
   Why're you here?

Jennifer
   Oh. Got tired of bumming around from job to job. After the last one, I thought a change would be good.

Lee
   What was the last one?

Jennifer
   Cotton candy taste tester.

Janet
   Doesn't sound so bad.

Jennifer
It wasn't, until a batch of fiberglass insulation got mixed in with an order. Thought I'd die.

Stephany
I see your point.

Jennifer
But on the upside, I haven't had to floss for nearly a year.

Stephany *(to Janet)*
And Brooklyn's here because…?

Janet
I'd rather not say.

Lee
Oh, come on! The rest of us told.

Jennifer
Yeah! Give!

Janet
Well, I can't go into too many details.

Stephany
I get it! You're on the lam!

Janet *(looking around)*
Sssh!

Stephany *(quieter; others gather round)*
You can trust us. We're buddies.

Lee
Our hips are sealed.

Jennifer
Lips!

Lee
> Huh?

Jennifer
> Our **lips** are sealed.

Lee
> Really? Wait here. I've got some chapstick in my bag.

Stephany
> Never mind! Just watch out for a sergeant. *(to Janet)* Come on, Brooklyn, out with it.

Janet
> OK, but if this gets out I'm screwed.

Jennifer
> Not to worry.

Janet
> You guys ever heard of…P.E.T.E.R.?

Lee *(raising her hand)*
> Oooh, I have! Pick me, pick me!

Stephany
> How did you ever find your way here from Kansas?

Lee
> Well, it was easy after the nice man in Montana turned my map right side up.

Jennifer
> People for the Ethical Treatment of the Everyday Rat? You actually belong to that bunch of crazies?

Janet
> Crazy is as crazy does. At least I've never eaten insulation.

Jennifer
Hey, Little Miss Know-It-All, I can eat ice cream now without my teeth hurting! So there!

Lee
Why is my brain hurting?

Stephany
The same reason your foot hurts when it's asleep. Everybody shut the hell up and let her talk. Go ahead, Janet.

Janet
I was the Brooklyn Intercity Taskmaster for Critter Health.

Jennifer
You were the B.I.T.C.H.?

Janet
With a capital B, honey. I was in charge of Rat Rescue for all five boroughs. And when our esteemed mayor held a press conference to announce his new District Initiative for Rodent Elimination and Selectively Transmitted Rat and Insect Termination System—

Jennifer (*pondering this*)
Umm…

Stephany
Wait a minute, let me think…

Lee
Oooh! I got it! D.I.R.E. S.T.R.A.I.T.S.! This is fun!

Janet
Well…I just had to do something! So I mobilized my crack team of Compassionate Humans United to Mitigate Political Stupidity.

Jennifer
There's an apropos anagram.

Stephany
    What'd you do, shoot somebody?

Jennifer
    Run 'em over with a Buick?

Lee
    Write a letter to the editor?

Janet
    Oh, no...we're a **serious** organization. Half-measures wouldn't do. We moved in under cover of darkness, using the most advanced tactical maneuver techniques, fully-camouflaged, and we—

Jennifer
    Cut the mayor's throat?

Stephany
    Scalped him?

Jennifer
    Castrated him?

Lee
    What's that?

Stephany
    What part of Kansas are you from, anyway?

Janet
    —We creamed him!

Jennifer
    Yeah, but how?

Janet
    I just said. We creamed him.

Stephany
What? Literally?

Janet
And thoroughly. Seven fully-loaded banana cream pies, right in the kisser. Just as the press conference cameras started rolling. It was glorious!

Stephany *(after a pause)*
You know, you may just be too tough for this outfit.

Janet
I'm hoping I can learn to tone down my aggressive tendencies here.

Jennifer *(to Stephany)*
OK, that's her story. That just leaves you. What's an independent babe like you doing going through boot camp?

Stephany
Simple. Family tradition.

Lee
Huh?

Stephany
For 200 years the eldest child in our family has gone into the service. I wasn't about to break that long proud line.

Jennifer
200 years?

Stephany
Damn right. My ancestors have been at all the tough ones. The brutal ones. The ones where few came back in one piece.

Janet
Even...the Big One?

Stephany
Especially the Big One. My granddad did three tours, starting in '42.

Jennifer
Wow! Europe?

Stephany
Of course. Italy. France. Belgium. Ended up in Berlin.

Lee
Did he teach you anything?

Stephany
You bet. **Everything.**

Janet
Everything? Really? Even…

Stephany
Even how to kill 'em. I can bust 'em up, believe me.

Jennifer
Whew! Unbelievable.

Stephany
I especially like it when they turn red in the face and can't breathe.

Lee
Ick!

Stephany
Honey, if you're gonna be in this outfit with us, you can't be squeamish. Millions expect it of you. They're depending on you.

Lee
I guess. I'll try my best.

Janet
Good for you!

Jennifer *(puts her hand out)*
All together then? No quitters?

Lee *(puts her hand in)*
No quitters!

Janet *(puts her hand in)*
No quitters!

Stephany *(puts her hand)*
No quitters!

(Whistle blows offstage. All four jump to attention. Everyone but Jennifer has a ridiculously exaggerated smile)

Stephany
Here we go! Stay tough!

*(**SERGEANT CHUCKLES** enters from DR. She is in full clown regalia: wig, nose, makeup, shoes, the works. She has a whistle around her neck and holds a long skinny balloon animal under an arm as if it is a riding crop. She wears a t-shirt that reads YUCK and carries a clipboard)*

Chuckles
All right, you pathetic wanna-be's! Heels together! Backs straight! Eyes front! *(stops in front of Jennifer)* What's the matter with you, private?

Jennifer
Nothing, ma'am!

Chuckles

Well, wipe that grin onto your face!

(Jennifer runs her hand across her mouth and grins till it hurts)

Chuckles

That's more like it! Can't go into combat with a frown. You'll have all those little kids crying their eyes out. *(pacing back and forth across the line)* My name is Seltzer-Sergeant Chuckles. I will be your drill instructor for the duration of your stay at Yankovick's Urban Clown Kamp. Years from now, thanks to my brutal, but fair, instruction, you will be able to say with pride, "I crawled through the muck with Chuck at YUCK!" When a tiny tot asks you where you received your devastating clowning skills, you can kneel down and tell her, "YUCK!" And when someone offers you a corn dog or an elephant's ear, you will think back fondly to our mess hall—and I do mean **mess** hall—and reply, "YUCK!" DO YOU UNDER-STAND?!

All Recruits

Ma'am, yes, ma'am!!

Chuckles

For the next few weeks I will be your mother, I will be your father, I will be your annoying Uncle Fred with the joy buzzer, dribble glass, and the saran wrap over your toilet. We will eat together, sleep together, train together. When you put on that silly wig, I'll be there. When you don your size 27EEEEE shoes, I'll be there. When you give your fellow recruit an atomic wedgie, believe you me, I will be there. And when that proud day arrives when you finally walk across the parade ground, clad in your dress plaid uniform, and the Kamp Commandant, Colonel Wheezie, glues on your red nose with special honking feature that marks you as a YUCK graduate…I'll be there, too.

You'll hate me, you'll despise me, you'll wish desperately that someone would just whack me with a giant foam rubber hammer...but in the end, you'll respect me and thank me for preparing you for the ultimate challenge of an enormous tent full of screaming, spoiled, stinky little munchkins. ARE YOU LISTENING TO ME?!

All Recruits
Ma'am, yes, ma'am!!

Chuckles (looking at clipboard)
All right. Now here's a rundown of this week's instruction. Commit it to memory and make sure you're there on time.

Monday: Makeup essentials. You will be required to apply clown white one-handed while looking in the rear-view mirror of a 1971 Chevrolet Vega that is speeding through heavy traffic. This will prepare you for the inevitable day when you oversleep and are late for two simultaneous children's birthday parties.

Tuesday: Wig basics. This will be your introduction to all the subtleties of nuance available in the wacky world of clown coiffure.

Wednesday: Obstacle course. You will proceed along an alley leading to a mock convention center, avoiding potholes, drunks, and bill collectors. Once inside, you will maneuver through crowds of autograph seekers, taking care not to complain that they are seeking the trapeze artists' autographs and not yours. You will climb to the top row of the seating area, smoke a forbidden cigar, then sprint to the dressing room ahead of the circus manager's wife, who simply will not leave you alone. After making up with someone else's kit, yours having been appropriated for the elephants, you will pursue your costume, which is being dragged around the center ring by one of the dancing poodles. After securing your tasteful yet amusing outfit, you will make the final dash to your tiny car, hurdling sleeping camels and diminutive horsies.

Thursday: Firing range. Rapid-fire seltzer bottle, ping-pong ball spitting, and fully-automatic silly string. Once you have mastered these awesome, albeit hilarious, Weapons of Mess Destruction you will proceed to water balloon mortars and the 13-kiloton confetti bomb. ARE YOU MOTIVATED, MAGGOTS?!

All Recruits

Ma'am, yes, ma'am!!

Chuckles

Friday: Your introduction to the M-2 Goofy Clowning Assault Vehicle, the most devastating 1-cylinder projection of comic power ever devised by the hand of man.

Upon the completion of your training you will be able to fit a fully-equipped platoon of 37 clowns inside. For God's sake, don't set off the airbag.

Saturday: You will draw your dopey shoes and YUCKsack for a 25-block parade march. Any recruits who fall out will pull extra KP duty, along with their entire luckless squad, in the Pie Shed. Don't let your buddies down.

Sunday: The Chaplain, Major Giggles, will address the company. I'm told his sermon will be "Blessed Are the Silly, For They Will Inherit A Saturday Morning Major-Market Children's Show."

CAN I GET AN 'OO-RAH'?!

All Recruits

Oo-rah!!

Chuckles

But before you can train with the best you'll have to be in top physical condition. A flabby clown may be a funny clown, but this outfit's HMO frowns on quintuple bypasses.

Lee

Sgt. Chuckles! Question, ma'am!

Chuckles

Spit it out, troop.

Lee

What's an HMO, ma'am?

Chuckles
Hilarity Maintenance Organization. Now zip your lip and prepare for Physical Training. Extended formation...move!

(Recruits extend both arms and spread out. Chuckles drops clipboard and gestures with balloon)

Chuckles
Pigeon-toed walk...!

All Recruits
Pigeon-toed walk...!

Chuckles
Step!

(Recruits do goofy splay-footed walk in place, complete with appropriate arm movements and facial expressions)

Chuckles
You call that a funny walk? I call it pathetic! Pick up those heels! Swing those elbows! *(to Lee)* Private, you need to get with the program!

Lee
Yes, sir!

Chuckles
Who you calling 'sir'? I'm a Seltzer-Sergeant! I **work** for a living! Drop and give me ten!

(Lee leans down, palms on floor, knees bent, head up. Chuckles winds up and whacks her on the rear end with the balloon)

Lee
One, Sergeant! *(this continues up to ten)*

Chuckles
Back in formation!

Lee
Yes, Sergeant! *(she rejoins recruits)*

Chuckles
Halt! *(recruits stop, come to attention)* Looney-face position...move!

(Recruits move feet shoulder-width apart. Hands go up beside their ears, palms out elbows low. Facial expressions are blank)

Chuckles
Ready...one!

(Recruits make ludicrous, silly facial expressions. Elbows are raised to the level of their ears. Fingers splay. Tongues come out, eyes pop. Knees bend in to till they touch)

Chuckles
Relax!

(Recruits return to original positions)

Chuckles
Two!

(Recruits make funny faces again. This continues up to a count of eight)

Chuckles *(to Lee)*
Troop, I don't think you're taking this seriously! I don't think you know what silly is! I've seen funnier faces on Mount Rushmore! Drop and give me ten!

(Lee assumes her former punishment posture and gets another balloon thumping, counting all the while as before. Other recruits are frozen in the silly-face position)

Chuckles
Back in formation! Everyone relax! Shake it out!

(Recruits stretch, behaving as if they've just run ten miles)

Chuckles
Squad...atten-tion!

All Recruits
We like it! We love it! We want more of it! More sill-**ee**, Drill Sergeant, more sill-**ee**!

Chuckles
Pair off!

(Stephany and Lee get together, facing each other. Janet and Jennifer do the same)

Chuckles
Clown cruelty position…move!

(Each pair squares off, one hand raised by each recruit)

Chuckles
Thirty seconds…move!

(Recruits perform matching Three Stooges routines, complete with vocalizations)

Chuckles
That's it! Don't hold back! Give it everything you've got! We're preparing you for Big Top Combat! *(to Lee)* Doesn't look to me like your heart's in this, Troop! I don't see the fire! My grandma does better eye jabs with her mascara bottle! Drop and give me **fifty**!

Lee
Yes, Sergeant!

(She assumes the punishment position again. Chuckles raises the balloon to strike)

Chuckles
One!

Stephany *(grabbing the balloon)*
Hey, leave her alone!

Chuckles

Troop, you better get back in formation or you'll be in a world of serious hurt!

Stephany

Why don't you stop picking on the kid? She's trying her best.

Chuckles

Well, maybe her best isn't good enough for this outfit. Maybe she needs some extra motivation.

Stephany

Maybe she just needs you to back off a little.

Chuckles *(pointing to her nose)*

You see this? I got this on the front line, Troop! Going toe-to-toe with the **enemy**. Maybe when you've stared down twenty thousand spoiled kids on a sugar-high, **you** can give some orders.

Stephany

I'm giving one right now: leave her alone!

Chuckles

There's always one in every class…a tough-gal who needs a lesson. Have it your way. *(steps up to her)* You want a piece of me, Troop? You want to make me leave her alone?

Stephany

Damn right! Bring it on, Sarge!

(Chuckles moves UC to the shelves. She pulls off the tarp, revealing clown props)

Chuckles

Fine with me. I need a workout. What's your pleasure? *(takes out each as she names them)* Juggling clubs? Pool noodles? Feather pillows? Cream pies?

Stephany

Foam hammers.

Chuckles

Oh, I like you, kid. Hard-core. *(she pulls two enormous foam hammers from the shelf, hands one to Stephany)* Ready when you are.

(They move downstage, stretching and warming up. The other recruits move UC in front of the shelves, Lee in the middle)

Jennifer

Way to go, Lee. You're getting us all in trouble. We'll be cleaning the elephant stalls till the day we leave.

Lee

Hey, don't blame this on me!

Janet

Who **should** we blame, then?

Lee

I didn't ask her to stick up for me.

Jennifer

Well, if you weren't such a humorless loser she wouldn't have had to.

Lee

Why don't you two just kiss my…my…hynie!

Janet
How about we kick it instead?

(They continue to argue quietly while the other two fight)

Chuckles
I'm gonna knock some sense out of you.

Stephany
Hey, knock yourself out.

(They fight. It's as silly as can be, of course. In the middle of it, the other three go at it with pool noodles. The fight degenerates into a general melee: pillows, silly strings, etc. with a cream-pie finish. All five end up sprawled on the ground, a complete mess. Lee has defeated Janet and Jennifer)

Chuckles *(to Lee)*
Kid, it takes a big clown to admit she's wrong…you're freaking ridiculous. *(to Stephany)* You, too.

Lee
Thanks, Sarge.

Stephany
Thanks.

Chuckles *(standing)*
Let's go. Time for chow. They're serving Jello in Loony-Tunes cups tonight.

(All stand, start off DR)

Chuckles *(singing)*
I don't know but I've been told—!

All Recruits *(singing)*
I don't know but I've been told—!

Chuckles
—Our platoon's as good as gold!

All Recruits
—Our platoon's as good as gold!

Chuckles
Fool's gold!

All Recruits
Fool's gold!

Chuckles
FOOL'S GOLD!!

All Recruits
FOOL'S GOLD!!

(All are off except Jennifer and Lee)

Lee *(offering a fingerful of cream to Jennifer)*
Hey…does this taste…funny…to you?

(They exit. Fadeout)

FAIR WARNING

A play by Terry Kroenung
© 2003

<u>SCENE</u>: *An exclusive auction house.*

<u>SET</u>: *Auctioneer's lectern, SR. Half a dozen padded wooden chairs SL, facing auctioneer. An enclosed case, like an armoire, is against the wall DL. Entrance UC for assistant to bring in sale items. The room is elegantly-appointed: carpets, drapes, etc.*

The seats are full. The patrons—four women, two men—are in evening dress and hold catalogs for the sale. The auctioneer, **MS. PURCHASE,** *stands at the lectern. She is in her 30's, crisp, handsome, wears glasses.*

Purchase

Good evening, ladies and gentlemen, and welcome to Ricasso's, the nation's preeminent invitation-only fine arts auction house. My staff informs me that all of your admittedly unorthodox pre-sale paperwork has been completed, so we are nearly ready to begin. My name is Elaine Purchase. I will be your guide for tonight's event, which we confidently declare to be the most comprehensive of its kind ever seen in this country. Even the famous auction of the LeQuillon daggers in 1926 pales in comparison to our exclusive offering here.

As you can see by the most cursory examination of your catalogs, we have had the immense good fortune to acquire the renowned DiGrassi Collection of medieval and Renaissance weaponry and associated articles. Consisting of one hundred thirty-seven pieces, the collection contains some of the finest examples of the swordcutler's art to be seen outside of a handful of major museums. The notorious eccentric Lorenzo DiGrassi spent a lifetime using his family's immense lima bean fortune to amass what is without a doubt the most wondrous private holding of this type imaginable. Following the tragic premature passing of this visionary last year to terminal flatulence, his grieving family decided to honor the unusual terms of his will, which was found behind a potted plant in a little-used room of his great mansion, Sans Sophia. The will mandated the sale of the collection to a most-exclusive group of bidders with whom DiGrassi had had dealings over the years. I would like to introduce those lucky few now.

In the front row, from the Parisian couture house of Du Foible, purveyors of elegance to the elite of three continents for nearly three centuries, we have Ms. **DAPHNE DU FOIBLE**. Her spring line of evening wear, based on a liberal use of yak hair and an even more liberal interpretation of "evening", caused a sensation in Milan this year. She is a respected expert on 17th century ivory codpieces. We are delighted to have her with us tonight.

Sitting beside her is **SCHLOMO BEN TANG**, heir to the largest family of kosher vintners in Japan. Mr. Tang has authored a definitive eleven-volume series on the history of medieval Norwegian pomanders, as you are doubtless aware. Welcome, Mr. Tang.

To his right is Miss **CARMEN ESCRIME**, beloved international philanthropist, who has used the proceeds from the sale of her medicinal fiber company, Lax Factor, to do immeasurable good around the world. We are all, of course, familiar with her selfless crusade to provide clutch purses to Third World orphans. Less well-known, perhaps, is that she is a noted authority on Renaissance halberd tassels. Miss Escrime…an honor.

At the end of the second row is **JUANITA MARIA CONCHITA ISABELLA PUNTO-REVERSO**, famed explorer of the darkest reaches of the Amazon Basin whose exploits were chronicled in her unforgettable best-selling memoir *Up the River of Death Without a Paddle*. Ms. Punto-Reverso is, of course, also considered the greatest living expert on Siberian blowgun art. A pleasure, madame.

(becoming flustered)

Escorting her is a man who scarcely needs an introduction, so widespread is his fame as international bon vivant. **PEDRO ESPADA-ROPERA**'s devastatingly handsome face and rugged physique have graced the cover of nearly every major periodical on earth, from *People* and *Newsweek* to *Gentleman's Quarterly* and *Vegetarian Times*. He was voted one of the World's Most Beautiful Cads by *Ms. Magazine*, the *Christian Science Monitor*, and *Women's Wear Daily*. Owner of extensive real estate holdings in his native Uruguay, he represented his country in the most recent Olympic Games as captain of the sabre team. I am happy to report that the most serious charges resulting from that affair have been recently settled out of court. You have no idea what a dream come true it is to have you here, Senor.

And last but not least, rounding out our sextet of discriminating buyers, we have Ms. **ROXANNE FLECHE**, star of such memorable cinematic classics as *The Mattress of Zorro, The Adventures of Disrobing Hood, The Corsucking Brothers,* and *The Man with the Iron Willie*. I believe that I can state, without fear of contradiction, that her collection of Bulgarian shackles, riding crops, and ball gags has no peer in the industrialized world. Ms. Fleche, my feelings at having you at my sale are…indescribable.

Now that the introductions are complete, we will proceed with the auction, after a short break so that our capable staff may ensure that all items are properly prepared for your viewing. Please take this time to go over your planned bids in your mind and make any mental preparations which may be required for your participation in this unique once-in-a-lifetime event.

(She exits through the UC door. The patrons look through their catalogs, speaking in isolated conversations

Foible *(French accent; 30's; snooty, absurdly well-dressed)*
She wears her clothes like stevedore.

Fleche *(standing, stretching; Californian, mid-20's; wearing as little as the occasion permits; fanning herself with the catalog)*
Oh, I don't know. I like stevedores. Sounds like a great name for one of my co-stars. Steve Adore. Long blonde hair. Perfect tan. Icy blue eyes. Pecs out to here. Tattoo of a rearing cobra on his—

Escrime *(40's; Texas twang; prudish, conservative, dim)*
Will he...be as accomplished a—um, performer as you?

Fleche *(teasing her)*
Honey, as long as his credentials are solid and he's a hard worker, that's all that matters.

Escrime *(innocently)*
Indeedy? I suppose you're always open to new prospects?

Fleche
Honey, you have no idea. I have exhausting auditions.

Reverso *(to Ropera; she is in her early 30's; exotic; Latin American accent)*
So you think I should go after the bastard sword?

Ropera *(30's; classic Latin lover type; very smooth)*
As one of my continent's most revered bastards, I could hardly suggest a different course.

Reverso
You're horrible.

Ropera
So it has been said.

Reverso
So you think this one is worth having?

Ropera (*stroking her neck*)
I would never waste my time with something not worth...having.

Reverso
You recommend I spend my money on it then?

Ropera
I do.

Reverso
Those are two words I never hoped to hear from your lips.

Ropera
You and a few dozen other beautiful women, cara mia.

Reverso
Oh, now I'm beautiful? Last night I was merely "an exotic jungle cat".

Ropera (*kissing her hand*)
You could never be "merely" anything, my tigress. I still ache from your caresses.

Reverso
I think I will purchase the bastard sword. And tonight, I may also purchase a sore bastard.

Ropera (*kissing her neck*)
Does the velvet scabbard come with that?

Reverso (*giggling*)
You're horrible.

Ropera
So it has been said.

Tang (*standing; 40's; elegant*)
I hope they speed things up. I have reservations at Capo Ferro's.

Foible
I have reservations <u>*about*</u> Capo Ferro's.

Tang
You do not respect their cuisine?

Foible
Do not misunderstand me. I find their sushi shish kebob fricassee flambe to be both picturesque and piquant. I also enjoy their signature dessert of pan-blackened earthworms smothered in a succulent caraway caramel sauce and topped with a circumcised radish. But they dress their staff like Ethiopian farmhands.

Tang
You are a slave to your unfailing fashion sense, Madame.

Foible
All too true. I make a tremendous effort to be forgiving to my benighted inferiors, but it is—how do you say?—a curse, and I must speak out.

Escrime (*reading catalog*)
Beg everyone's pardon, but why do they call it a ballock dagger?

Fleche (*laughing*)
Come here, honey. I'll explain it to you. I have a visual aid in my bag.

Ropera (*sharing a smile with all the others*)
If I may, good lady. The name comes from Sir Demetrius Ballock, the great British cricketer of the 19th century. He once scored 225 not out, while taking six wickets as slow bowler, against a fearsome Lithuanian team. In recognition of this tremendous achievement his club gave him a specially-designed dagger, engraved with his

achievement and the date in 24-carat gold. Ever since, this type of dagger has been called a ballock.

Escrime
Why, thank you, sir.

Ropera
Not at all. *(sits)*

Reverso *(repressing a laugh)*
It took some impressive ballocks to tell that ridiculous story.

Ropera
High praise, indeed, coming from you, Madame.

Reverso
You were tres cruel.

Ropera
I repeat my earlier response.

Reverso
May I put in for an order of that cruelty myself, for late evening delivery?

Ropera
I shall clear my calendar.

Tang *(to Escrime)*
Permit me…I understand that you are a philanthropist?

Escrime
Why, yes. Only in a small way, though. No enormous foundation—

Foible *(to herself)*
Except on her face.

Escrime

—But there was a tidy sum left when I sold Daddy's business to that big conglomerate.

Tang

Oh, your laxative company. Ms. Purchase mentioned that? You were no longer interested in it?

Escrime

Lordy, no. Never could stomach it. Takes a lot of guts to stick it out in the corporate world.

Tang

I would certainly concur.

Escrime

Daddy always used to say, "Little Prune"—that was what he always used to call me, Little Prune—"my whole life has been bound up in this company. I can't relax, not for a minute."

Tang

He sounds like he was quite a man.

Escrime

Oh, he was, he was. But in the end he was just a regular guy.

Tang

Indeed.

Escrime

And what about you? I hear you make kosher wine?

Tang

We do. The largest winery in Asia. I am very proud of the fact that we were able to persuade the revered Rabbi Fujimoto to give us our slogan.

Escrime

And what is it?

Tang
"Business is always bris-k!"

Escrime
I'm sorry. I'm afraid I don't grasp that.

Tang
I can well believe it *(to Fleche)* Oy!

Fleche
I can grasp it.

Tang
I can well believe it. Business brisk, is it?

Fleche
You have no idea. *(whispers)* That goes double for her.

(Purchase enters UC, proceeds to her lectern)

Purchase
My apologies for the delay, ladies and gentlemen. We had some last-minute adjustments to make and we wanted to make sure your release forms were in order. Ricasso's prides itself on the most exclusive, if not positively secretive, arrangements in the industry. Frequently that requires a little extra time to get it right. But the doors are bolted and guarded, the Emergency Medical Technicians are on stand-by, and the year's most eagerly-awaited auction can now begin.

*(Lighting change. **MS. FORTE**, the lovely young assistant, enters UC with an ornate Gothic mace. She holds it up for the patrons to inspect)*

Purchase *(as patrons gather around Forte at C)*

Item 1 from the Ricasso Collection: the war mace of Bishop Bernard, Fighting Priest of Schleswig-Holstein. As you know, the clergy often used maces in battle to evade the metaphorical Biblical proscription against men of the cloth "shedding blood with the edge of the sword". This particular specimen has an interesting history. Bishop Bernard was actually dispatched with it by a Mrs. Schiller when she caught the man of God administering decidedly unorthodox rites to her eleven year-old son in the vestry.

We will start the bidding at DiGrassi's reserve price of $30,000. Please prepare your bids in accordance with the special instructions in your catalog, reprinted from the great man's handwritten will. Those not taking part in this round are advised to watch for flying bids.

(Ropera and Reverso return to their seats. Escrime, Tang, Fleche, and Foible move to the SL cabinet, where they each procure a rapier. They arrange themselves into a semicircle at C, facing downstage)

Purchase

Very good. Bidding will be in $500 increments only, starting at $30,000. First bid?

(Tang salutes with his sword)

Purchase

Mr. Tang. Very good. Mr. Tang bids $30,000. Do we have 30,500?

(Fleche attacks, Tang parries)

Purchase
Ms. Fleche at 30-and-5. 32?

(Foible attacks, Fleche parries)

Purchase
Ah, Ms. Foible has her eyes on the prize. 32-5?

(Tang attacks Foible; Escrime jumps in, and the fight becomes a 4-way affair)

Purchase *(throwing in bids as things get frisky)*
This bodes well for our evening. Spirited bidding on the very first item.

(Fight concludes. Tang wins the mace as the others gradually salute and drop out)

Purchase
Mr. Tang at $54,000. Anyone else? Fair warning. $54,000. And...sold to Mr. Schlomo Ben Tang. Well done!

(Polite applause from the other patrons; Forte exits UC to bring out the next item)

Ropera
I believe this is the weapon you lust after, my lady.

Reverso *(eyeing him)*
And will you give it to me?

Ropera *(standing)*
  I shall do my best to give satisfaction. *(crosses to cabinet, selects a sword)* $150,000 maximum, you said?

Reverso
  That is my limit today.

Ropera
  You may have to raise it later.

Reverso
  I was hoping you'd say that.

Purchase *(as Forte brings out bastard sword)*
  Item 2: the incomparable hand-and-a-half of Prince Pedro the Cross-Eyed, found still clutched in his lifeless hand after the Battle of Reluctant Virgins in 1386. Witnesses were quoted as saying that Pedro, living up to his nickname to the very last, tragically stabbed right when he should have stabbed left.
  Reserve price on this magnificent weapon is $110,000. Please prepare your bids carefully.

(Fleche and Ropera are the only bidders. They salute at C)

Purchase
  Opening bid at 110?

(Ropera salutes)

Purchase *(watching him as a mouse watches a hawk)*
  The splendid Senor Espada-Ropera opens the bidding.

(Fleche attacks. The two go at it in fine style, making full use of all of their erotic charms. As Purchase calls a bid on each attack she becomes visibly more excited. The fight reaches an ecstatic, panting paused, corps-a-corps at $150,500)

Purchase
$150, 500, Ms. Fleche. Mr.Tang? Fair warning at $150,500…

*(Ropera kisses Fleche in the frozen corps-a-corps. She responds as only she can. Purchase is about to wet herself. Reverso is decidedly **not** amused. Mid-kiss Ropera binds Fleche's rapier down with his, gets behind her, blade to her throat)*

Purchase *(whimpering)*
Senor Ropera, a…breathtaking bid of 151. Ms. Fleche? Fair warning at 151.

(Fleche grimaces, shakes her head, relaxes)

Fleche
That's twice I've lost tonight.

Ropera *(for her ears only)*
The night is still young. Perhaps you will prevail later.

Fleche
You have a mighty thrust, sir.

Ropera
You have no idea.

Purchase *(as they separate)*
Sold to Senor Espada-Ropera, acting for Ms. Punto-Reverso, at $151,000. Congratulations!

(Applause as the fighters sit)

Reverso *(snippishly)*
I presume you're good for the extra $1,000?

Ropera
I was thinking of payment in kind, actually.

Reverso *(still sour, eyeing Fleche)*
You think you'll have the reserves for that?

Ropera *(kissing her neck)*
That's why I make deposits, my lady.

Reverso *(smiling, despite herself)*
Horrible.

Purchase *(drinking water and fanning herself)*
I think we may all agree that that was a thrilling exchange. Worthy of the late Mr. DiGrassi. Now if Ms. Forte will bring out the next article…

(Forte exits UC)

Foible
Finally, something worth bidding on.

Purchase *(as Forte returns with a pair of embroidered gloves)*
Item 3: a truly one-of-a-kind specimen. The dueling gloves of Lady Helena DuPrique, legendary London swordswoman who, custom states, was never bested in single combat. Finest white kid,

with intricate green-and-gold embroidery on the cuffs that might have been done by elven magicians. Tradition has it that the red-brown stain on the middle finger there is the blood of her lover, the scandalous Viscount Vincent le Vayne. It was left there as his life-blood poured out onto a Mayfair street in 1601 when the happy couple was ambushed by assassins sent by the anguished Lord DuPrique, who has stood all that a man could be reasonably expected to stand. Lady Helena could not save her beloved, despite sending three of his assailants to perdition. In mourning till the day she, too, passed over to the Elysian Fields, Lady Helena ended her days pining away for Lord Vayne at the Convent of the Seven Sanctified Sinners, now the Monte Carlo Casino.

Escrime
Isn't that romantic?

Fleche
Honey, you need to learn how to read between the lines.

Foible *(standing)*
I will have those gloves at any price.

Fleche *(moving toward her)*
Over my dead bootie.

Foible *(lifting sword)*
It will be as dead as your fashion sense.

Ropera *(standing)*
Well, then…

Reverso *(pushing him back down and standing)*
I think not. No more sending a boy to do a woman's job. *(takes his rapier)* May I borrow your weapon?

Ropera
That would depend on where you plan to stick it.

Reverso
In your Fleche.

Purchase
We will start at $14,000.

(All women gather at C)

Purchase
Ah! The ladies have an eye for the finery this evening. May I presume that Madame Foible will open the bidding?

Foible
You may.

Purchase
Well, then…we are at $14,000.

(The fight is a catty frenzy. Purchase can barely keep up with her announcement of the bids. Escrime drops out, wounded in the hand. Tang tends to her UR with his handkerchief. Foible, Fleche, and Reverso continue apace. Foible is knocked semi-conscious DL. Forte tends to her with a suddenly-produced medical bag. The remaining pair are a tornado of blades at C. They end up climactically skewering each other stone-cold dead)

Purchase
And *that* is the kind of bidding that separates the women from the boys. Gentlemen, you have much to learn about product acquisition. If we could have a moment of silence, please, for a pair of truly admirable shoppers. *(pause)* We are at $38,500. Ms. Foible, it

appears that you are the winning bidder. Your competitors have…er, cancelled one another out. Lady Helena's gory gauntlets are yours. Well-done!

(Foible stands and limps toward Purchase; as she steps over the intertwined bodies at C, she stops and looks down at Reverso)

Foible
Lovely scarf. *(to Ropera)* May I?

(Ropera shrugs. She stoops, removes Reverso's red scarf, examines it)

Foible
It has little piranha fish embroidered on it. How sweet. *(to Ropera)* Her family crest, perhaps?

Ropera
You have no idea.

(Foible sits. Tang moves to help Escrime to her seat. Ropera moves to the lectern)

Escrime
I knew this crazy auction might get someone hurt, but I never thought anyone would get killed.

Tang
As the Revered Rabbi Fujimoto always says to us, "Life. Go figure." How are you, madame?

Escrime
Sliced my hand something awful. If I'd had a glove on, it wouldn't have happened. Byronic, huh?

Tang
I think you mean *ironic*.

Escrime
Do I? *(winces)* This really hurts.

Tang
Permit me. *(hands her a pocket flask)*

Escrime
Why, thank you. The family label?

Tang
Of course. Chateau Tang.

Escrime *(sips)*
Oooh! Tastes orangey.

Tang *(sighs)*
Go figure.

Purchase
Senor, we have a situation here.

Ropera
Who is paying for Pedro's sword?

Purchase
Precisely. I thought as her champion you could—

Ropera
Alas, madam, you find me separated from my checkbook this evening.

Purchase

Ah…what a pity. *(removes her glasses)* You know, as Ricasso's official representative, I am authorized to approve all…alternative payment options.

Ropera

What, like arm-wrestling me for it?

Purchase

Something like that.

Ropera

You intrigue me, Ms. Purchase. I took you for a cold, clinical woman who played by the book.

Purchase *(drawing very close to him)*

I'm a woman who wants to book a room, play, and be taken, Senor.

Ropera

And by "play", what exactly might you mean? Poker?

Purchase

Something like that. It might interest you to know that when you filled out your liability waiver forms, next-of-kin notifications, and wills before agreeing to our special event here, I did very well by the late lamented Ms. Fleche and her collection of Bulgarian…artifacts.

Ropera

Well, well! I see that you are one of that new breed of enlightened American women who refuse to be chained by tradition.

Purchase

We take pains to live life without restraint.

Ropera

Could you not whip up some enthusiasm for a little restraint?

Purchase
The idea doesn't make me gag,

Foible *(jumping up, exasperated)*
Mon dieu! Will you two just get a room?! The auction is clearly over, anyway. If I understand the rules.

Purchase
Clearly. By the terms set down by Mr. DiGrassi, it ended at first blood.

Foible
Then I shall collect my gloves from the sales office and take them downtown to display in my window. Would it be gauche of me to inquire as to who is going to clean up this mess?

Purchase
Ms. Forte, I think it is time you alerted Security to activate the End-of-Auction Disposal Protocol. *(to patrons)* Ricasso's enjoys impeccable relations with several prestigious medical schools, to say nothing of every hot dog vendor in the city.

Foible
So this happens here on a regular basis?

Purchase
You have no idea.

(Foible exits UC with Forte)

Tang *(escorting Escrime DL)*
I will get you a cab and then come back for my mace. Which hotel are you at again?

Escrime
The Wannamaker. *(they exit DL)*

Ropera
Why would anyone name a four-star hotel after a crass locker room comment?

Purchase
Wannamaker?

Ropera
No, she's not my type. Perhaps some other time.

Purchase
The gossip is all too true. You *are* horrible.

Ropera
It is a family trait. It is perhaps why we are such a large family. And what about you? Are you horrible? *(laughs)* Are you secretly planning to tether me to your enormous four-poster bed and worship my fevered flesh with the kiss of your whip?

(Purchase draws him close, slowly and tenderly. Then she grasps his hand in a one-handed wrist lock. He falls to his knees, whimpering, face on a chair, looking downstage. She places a stiletto-heeled shoe on the chair, next to his anguished face)

Purchase
Kiss it, Senor.

Ropera *(grimacing)*
What is this, Madame?

Purchase
"Mistress". This is…fair warning.

(Fadeout)

IN RUSSET MANTLE CLAD

A play by Terry Kroenung
© 2003

<u>SCENE:</u> *A dueling ground, France, 1805; elsewhere in Misere's memories and fantasies.*

<u>SET:</u> *Open stage.*

(Two pairs of overcoated figures stand upstage, one UR and one UL, in silhouette. At C are two figures in breeches, shirt, and boots, also in silhouette. They are poised to begin a smallsword duel.

Music begins. The fight occurs in slow-motion; it is nevertheless realistic.

*A spot comes up DR on **MISERE**. She is dark, young; attractive enough but not a beauty queen. She looks like what she is: a victim of war and suffering. She wears a long dark-red cape over breeches, boots, and a blue hussar's jacket. As the fight and music continue she speaks)*

Misere

Misere. What a name to give a child. Aren't we supposed to be bundles of joy, the comfort of our parents in their dotage? All the poems say so. And yet, don't we enter this breathing world wailing, bloody packages of fear? I know that's how we leave it—at least, that's how most of my men leave it. Howling in scarlet agony for their mothers as Prussian shells burst around us. Well, Shakespeare said "we are born to die."

(The SR figure in the fight falls; the SL victor drops sword, cradles the loser tenderly)

Perhaps my mother was more of a philosopher than she knew.

(Upstage tableau blacks out)

When I left home, as much to escape the greasy hands of my new stepfather as to seek my fortune, she gave me this cape. My 'dowry', she called it. My 'trousseau' is more accurate. When I married Bonaparte—his army, at least—this is all I had of my own.

(She wraps the cape tightly around herself and moves left as the lights come up on the DL corner, where the SERGEANT, middle-aged and world-weary, sits at a small table)

Sergeant
  Name?

Misere
  Claude Montjoy.

Sergeant *(after a long look at her)*
  Place of birth?

Misere
  Anjou.

Sergeant
Age?

Misere
Nineteen. In March.

Sergeant
Are you here of your own free will?

Misere
I am.

Sergeant
You owe no debt? Are not a fleeing felon?

Misere
I am not.

Sergeant
Right. Raise your right hand. Do you know which one that is?

Misere
Does insult come with the Emperor's pay?

Sergeant
I mean no insult, boy. You'd be amazed how many yokels join up who don't know left from right...nor who their fathers are, I'll wager.

Misere *(raising right hand)*
My father was Arthur Montjoy.

Sergeant
Well, good for you. Listen carefully, this is the last time you get to make a decision for three years. "Do you swear by Almighty God to faithfully serve the Emperor and your sacred nation of France against all enemies, at peril to your life and immortal soul if you should fail in your trust?"

Misere
I do.

Sergeant (*holding out form and pen*)
Right. Make your mark here.

Misere (*taking pen*)
I can write. And read. (*signs form*)

Sergeant (*rolling his eyes*)
Oho! Aren't we the paragon! Officer material. That and five thousand francs will get you out of the mud, my boy.

Misere
Only five thousand?

Sergeant
Only? Do you have even _five_ francs?

Misere
Would I be here if I did?

Sergeant
Not likely. Can you ride?

Misere
A little.

Sergeant
You're about to ride a lot. 3ʳᵈ Hussars lost two companies last month. Report to Lieutenant Maitre. And Private Mountjoy...watch your back. He likes to...um, initiate the young ones into his troop. And with a name like yours, how could he resist?

(*Crossfade to SR. **MAITRE** is DR. He has a bleeding cheek, cut very deeply. **PIERRE** and **ALPHONSE**, fellow officers, are laughing. All are young, cocky, and wear hussar's uniforms*)

Pierre
At least he spared your pretty eyes.

Alphonse
I like him. He fights. That's more than most of my troop can say.

Maitre *(tossing and catching a gold coin; he does this throughout the play)*
Your commiseration with my plight touches me deeply.

Pierre
Looks like the boy touched you deeply.

Alphonse
Serves you right for trying to touch _him_ deeply.

Maitre
That's all right. I never saw an enemy position yet that I couldn't take.

Pierre
I don't think this one wants to assume the position you'd like him to.

Alphonse
In fact, I think it's safe to assume that the next time you attack his rear, you'll receive another frontal assault. He prefers to face his foe.

Pierre
Forget him, Victor. The army's full of boys.

Maitre *(grabbing him by the throat)*
I don't think I like your tone, my little Pierre. I'm not a boy-lover. It's just an initiation. That's all.

Alphonse *(hand on his shoulder)*
Maitre…

Maitre *(releasing Pierre)*
All right.

Alphonse *(to Pierre)*
Come on. Let's inspect the pickets.

Maitre
An initiation! Nothing more.

Pierre
As you say. *(exits DR with Alphonse)*

(Maitre touches his cheek, then follows them; fade out)

Misere *(revealed DL)*
No explaining it, really. He touched me, I fought. Very little thinking went into it. The moment I drew on him I knew that I was a swordsman. Power swelled my arm like air fills a balloon. He didn't take me seriously at first. Neither did I, truth be told. But it was as if I were born to the blade. Thirty seconds after it started we both realized that I was almost reading his mind. Nothing he tried could penetrate my guard. And my first flick opened up his cheek to the bone. I could smell the fear as his blood hit the air. And then he was gone.

He avoided me like the pestilence for weeks after that. Never gave me a direct order, never made a correction or a comment on my performance. But his sullen eyes burned into me day in and day out. It was liked being stalked by a high-flying falcon. I was a field mouse waiting to feel the fell shadow on my back.

It was easier to fool them than I'd expected. I pretended to be a shy church-going lad. Baths and calls of nature I attended to in the woods or behind a wall. I knew my luck couldn't last and the day would come when my little game would be end. But I was as surprised as anyone as to how the checkmate came about.

*(Lights full up on whole stage. Maitre and the Sergeant stand beside Misere. Alphonse, Pierre, and **ANGELIQUE** are facing them at SR. Angelique is white-blonde, slim, icy cool. She, too, is in disguise as a man)*

Maitre *(still tossing his coin)*

We have a point of military honor to uphold, that's all. My fellow officers over in B Troop claim that their newly-arrived Private Beauvais here is the best bladesman in the 3rd Hussars. I humbly submit that my own Private Mountjoy is ummatched in the entire division. So we have arranged a friendly exchange to determine the truth.

Misere

Sir, I do not desire to fight this man. Give me a real enemy to kill.

Maitre

Who said anything about killing? We merely play to first touch here. We even dulled these weapons. Just try not to put your eye out. The Colonel would have little sense of humor about that.

Pierre

Besides, there is no real enemy. The Emperor has them so in awe of us that they wet themselves whenever someone pops a cork on a bottle of French champagne.

Alphonse *(laughing)*

Leaves more for us, eh?

Maitre *(as Pierre and Alphonse help Angelique out of her jacket)*

And to whet the edge of your dull ardor, I've made special arrangement with a squad of brawny sergeants from the Pioneer Battalion: if you lose, you'll get your initiation in front of the entire regiment…with extreme vigor. Do we understand one another?

Misere

Perfectly, sir. But I have a condition of my own.

Maitre

I'm eager to hear it.

Misere

Five thousand francs.

Maitre

Excuse me?

Misere

If I humiliate him, you give me five thousand francs.

Maitre

You're not in an enviable bargaining position, Montjoy.

Misere

I disagree, sir. Who knows about that scar on your cheek but your two faithful friends there...and me? The scar that the rest of the regiment believes is a battle wound.

Maitre

You aim high. Beware...so did Icarus.

Misere

So did Bonaparte. Sir.

Maitre

I begin to like you, Private.

Misere

I fear I cannot say the same of you. But if events fall out in our favor, no one shall ever know the truth of how your handsome face was ruined.

Maitre

Ruined? I think it an improvement.

Misere

As you say. Do we have a bargain?

Maitre

Why not? It's only money. We may all be butchered tomorrow. What good would it be then? But you must **thrash** him. I'm not interested in winning on points.

Misere

I shall do my best to give satisfaction.

Maitre

Do. I expect to see him on his back, prey to your best thrusts.

Misere

Of course. And if you have any thoughts of betrayal, Lieutenant—

Maitre

Fear me not on that score. I have no delusions about my chances in a duel with you. Hell, I can't even win an argument here.

Misere

A good officer knows his limitations.

Maitre

As you say. An adage that applies to private soldiers as well.

Alphonse

Come on, Maitre. Are we going to fight or talk?

Pierre

I need to collect my winnings before the taverns close.

Maitre

You count your francs in your dreams, gentlemen. We are ready.

Pierre

The dream was yours, believing that you have a chance here. Forswear the poppy, Maitre.

Maitre
Let us see what transpires, my friends. Plenty of time to taunt each other then.

Alphonse
Take your positions, then.

(Angelique and Misere face off)

Alphonse
En guarde...allez!

(They fight. Angelique is crisp, clean, a fencing machine. Every move is textbook-perfect, but predictable. Misere is more extravagant and intuitive)

Pierre *(to Maitre)*
Do I see you holding your breath over there?

Maitre
No, you see me holding your money!

(The duelists come together violently on a failed fleche from Angelique. They push off to gain distance and freeze, staring at one another with sudden insight. The men do not notice)

Alphonse
Come on, Beauvais! Finish him!

Pierre
It's not polite to toy with your prey!

(Angelique forsakes her excellent form and charges in. Misere takes advantage of this to disarm and trip her. Angelique ends up on the ground, panting, with both sword points on her chest)

Misere
I will — Never fight in a red fog…sir.

Angelique
I will take your advice…sir.

(Fade out. Spot on Misere, DR)

Misere
One invitation postponed…another about to begin. While the officers marched off together to drink Maitre's winnings and debate the merits of the fight, I took advantage of the time to step into the trees and wash off the sword-sweat. *(She strips off her jacket and shirt, down to her bound bosom)* I wasn't as cautious as usual.

Angelique *(appearing behind her, also shirtless, but with her jacket thrown over her shoulders; she smokes a cigar)*
A pain in the ass, isn't it?

Misere *(freezes; does not turn)*
What is?

Angelique
The pretense. The lying.

Misere
Preferable to earning centimes on my back in some foul barn.

Angelique *(wryly)*
Not interested in a stable relationship? It's not so bad. "Close your eyes and think of France"...or at least someone worth screwing. You can get used to anything if the circumstances require it.

Misere
I can't argue with that.

Angelique
Thank you. Amateur philosophy is something of a hobby with me. Cigar?

Misere *(shaking her head)*
Is this *(gestures at her)* a hobby, too?

Angelique
Hell, no. This is self-preservation. I have a need for some temporary anonymity. You?

Misere *(shrugs)*
Food. A bed. A few francs. Seemed like the best course at the time.

Angelique
Ah...a man of simple needs.

Misere *(small laugh)*
So I thought.

Angelique
We can't do this much longer, you know.

Misere
I know. I'll be leaving as soon as—

Angelique
—As soon as you collect your five thousand from Maitre?

(Misere raises an eyebrow)

Angelique
Didn't I tell you? Mind-reading is another of my hobbies.

Misere
Or sorcery.

Angelique
If I had that skill it would have been you on the ground instead of me. No, I can't read minds. But I can read lips. Came in very handy backstage sometimes.

Misere
An actress. Should have known.

Angelique
Yes. And a damned good one, I don't mind saying. Truly pissed off my petty-noble family when I left with the touring company for a grand life of glamour, glitter, and greasepaint. I gather they felt that they could have more profitably invested the small fortune they'd spent on my elegant education. But it wasn't wasted. All that training turned out to be useful when I had to play quality. *(snorts)* Quality! I've seen more scum in satin and silk the last two years than I've ever seen in rags. Think their shit doesn't stink. Don't take it kindly when you help yourself to a few of their spare francs, either. Barely had time to grab a few clothes and a sword and high-tail it out of there ahead of the gendarmes.

Misere
And here you are. Promoted to private. Was fencing part of your elegant education?

Angelique *(laughs)*
Hardly. That I learned from a true master of the sword…in return for mastering his.

Misere *(smiles)*
Payment in kind.

Angelique
Well, I thought it was awfully kind of me.

Misere
Thought I was going to lose to you.

Angelique
That makes two of us. Serves me right for going in all too eager.

Misere
Easy to do.

Angelique
It won't happen next time.

Misere
There won't be a—

Angelique
Don't be too sure. Boys don't like to have their pride hurt. I'd count on a mandatory rematch.

Misere
I won't be here long enough to have to worry about that.

Angelique
Oh, yes! Your blessed five thousand! Bonaparte will abdicate before you see a sou of it.

Misere
You think Maitre is not a man of honor?

Angelique
He probably is among his fellows. But he likely won't feel bound to a promise made to one of his privates.

Misere

If he screws me I'm bound to cut off his privates...and he knows it.

Angelique

Oh, ho! So that's what you were saying to him with your back to me. I gather that pretty scar on his cheek came from you? At initiation time?

Misere

And you have no idea what a pleasure it was.

Angelique

I wasn't nearly as creative as you when my turn came. Just paid five hundred francs to forego the honor. Not that I would have necessarily have kicked and screamed anyway, except for dramatic effect.

Misere

Really?

Angelique

My fencing master prized his expertise very highly.

Misere

Aren't we broad-minded.

Angelique

Just practical. And it precluded the joys of motherhood as well. But a cavalry saddle is no place to savor that particular romantic novelty.

Misere (*winces*)

As you say. (*pause*) Are all men swine?

Angelique

So I hear. Mind you, I haven't...known them all.

(Both laugh)

Angelique
On the off-chance that you get the money from Maitre, what will you do with it?

Misere
I was thinking of buying a Lieutenant's commission with it.

Angelique *(rolling her eyes)*
Oh, please!

Misere
But after actually seeing some Lieutenants, I've decided that it would be a demotion.

Angelique
Hear, hear!

Misere
So I'll probably just desert and set up shop someplace. They'll never find Claude Montjoy, if they ever bother to look. All they'll find is poor Misere.

Angelique
Misere? There's truth in advertising.

Misere *(donning shirt)*
As you say.

Angelique
What would this shop sell?

Misere
Books, perhaps.

Angelique
Need a partner?

Misere
The elegantly-educated Monsieur Beauvais?

Angelique
No, the notorious actress Angelique Delacroix.

Misere
Angelique? *(laughs)* You aren't **that** good an actress.

Angelique *(donning jacket)*
Even Lucifer fell.

Misere
Misery and the Cross. There's a perfect combination.

Angelique
And a good name for a bookstore.

Misere
Please! I don't fancy starving the first month.

Angelique *(as Misere dons her cape)*
In Russet Mantle Clad, then? That'll draw the quality.

Misere
Very well, then. *(they shake hands)* Be ready to run on a moment's notice.

Angelique
Have no fear of that. I have a bag already packed.

(Angelique exits DR; Misere finishes buttoning her jacket)

Misere
As do I, my friend.

(she follows DR; the Sergeant is revealed behind them. He has heard and seen it all. He smiles and moves DL, where lights reveal Maitre. They converse silently. The Sergeant is paid. They exit DL. Spot reveals Misere DC)

Misere

Friend…not a word that had often left my lips before. I had probably said "Lithuanian" as often, and with as much conviction. Perhaps it was merely the bond of a shared peril, comprehensible to no man, but I felt drawn to Angelique as if she were a corsair, grappling my soul while preparing to board it. The sentiment was returned, and a good thing, too. We went on campaign to Germany the very next day. For weeks we rode like fiends, scouting for the Grand Armee, keeping its flanks safe. My charming Lieutenants spent as much time scouting the flanks of the local girls, but still riding like fiends. I could only protect a fraction of them. Angelique and I were too busy protecting each other. Twice she picked me up at a gallop when I had been unhorsed. Thrice I had killed Austrian dragoons who were about to backstab her. She joked that she owed me a life. I joked that she only owed me her horse.

We won at Austerlitz. If 35,000 dead and wounded on both sides is a victory. 35,000…the village I was born in only had thirty families in it. Bonaparte celebrated his masterpiece of generalship. His troops celebrated not being in the Austrian army. Angelique and I celebrated our impending escape to a life of bibliophilic freedom. *(pause)* That was premature. The Lieutenants chose this moment to hold their own special celebration.

(Lights come up on whole stage. The Sergeant and Maitre are at LC. Alphonse and Pierre are at RC, each holding Angelique by an arm. She has no jacket, only her shirt. Misere moves to C cautiously)

Maitre *(still tossing his coin)*
I was flushed with pride yesterday at our great success, particularly at the performance of our regiment. We lost some good men, yes, but the enemy lost more. Many more. The 3rd Hussars cut a scarlet swath of destruction through the ranks of the craven Austrians.

Misere *(sardonically)*
Vive la France.

Maitre
So imagine my distress at discovering that I had lost two of my best men. Or, to be more precise, that I had never had two men at all.

(Rips open Misere's jacket and tears her shirt, revealing her disguise. Angelique surges forward, but is restrained by her captors. Misere backhands Maitre, draws her sword. The Sergeant aims a pistol at her face. Pierre holds his to Angelique's head)

Maitre
You are a fine hand with a blade…Mademoiselle, but I doubt even you can parry a bullet. I invite you to try.

Misere
I invite **you** to draw your sword and step out here.

Maitre
I accept your challenge. But of course, as your social superior, I am forbidden to soil my blade on you.

Misere
Oh, come on. You can…turn the other cheek.

(Alphonse and Pierre laugh. Maitre's glare silences them)

Maitre
I'm afraid that's what you'll be screaming halfway through your upcoming, and long overdue, initiation. But I am getting ahead of myself.

Misere
I'm going to get your head **for** myself.

Maitre
Bold words should be backed by bold deeds, lady. Since you are so keen to fight, may I present my chosen representative? *(Pierre shoves Angelique forward)* The darling of the repertory stage, performing in her greatest—and sadly—final role...Angelique Delacroix.

Misere
Hiding behind a woman's steel? Is this the vaunted Hussar courage? What would the Colonel have to say about this, I wonder?

Maitre
It might be instructive to find out, but unfortunately our geriatric commander is at a party with Marshal Ney. Simply unavailable till morning, I'm afraid.

Misere
I will not give you the satisfaction. You want to watch women fight, crawl back to the brothel you were born in.

Maitre
Ohhh! Meow! If only your prospects for survival matched your tongue. You will fight, my haughty little bitch, or you will be shot dead where you stand.

Misere

You'll turn cold-blooded murderer just to soothe a wound to your pride?

Maitre

No, I will be doing my duty executing a pair of deserters. The Sergeant here saw and heard you planning it last month. Well within regulations.

Misere

Your sudden conversion to protector of the Armee's virtue is nothing short of miraculous.

Maitre

As would be your survival, were it to happen. Let's go. You have a duel to fight.

Misere

No. If we're dead anyway, why play your childish little game?

Maitre

You've been so deucedly charming, I haven't been able to get to the incentive. The loser of your exchange will...well, lose, and the winner will get a day's head start. I fancy a bit of hunting after our great victory.

Angelique

We're supposed to believe you'll keep your word?

Maitre

Ah, Alphonse, so little faith among the enlisted men these days. I worry for the future of the Armee.

Alphonse

As do I.

Pierre

How **will** the Empire survive?

Maitre

Not your problem. None of you will live to see the sunset.

(Lieutenants all laugh)

Alphonse

Didn't I say I liked him...her...from the first? She fights! Two pistols on her and still she fights!

Maitre

You've proved your point. You have balls after all. Much good may they do you. Sergeant, if she isn't fighting the other woman in ten seconds, shoot her.

(Maitre makes a move toward the Sergeant. Angelique stops her)

Angelique

Misere...no. Come on, let's give them a show.

Maitre

You misunderstand. There will be no "show". The moment I suspect either of you is not really trying to kill, we will shoot you both in the head. Give her your sword, Pierre.

(Pierre arms Angelique, steps UR with Alphonse. Maitre and the Sergeant step UL. Misere removes her cape, drops it downstage)

Angelique

You know, I never liked breeches roles. Too contrived.

Misere
Tough audience this morning.

Angelique
Well, the provincial crowds are always lacking in refinement.

Misere
Do your best. Don't give them a reason to shoot.

Angelique
As if they would need one.

Misere
Forget it's me.

Angelique
Close my eyes and think of France?

Misere
Or at least of someone worth skewering.

(Both laugh and salute)

Maitre
I'm glad you're amused. Now amuse **us**. The sun is coming up. Allez!

(They fight. They do not hold back. After several spirited exchanges, they end up in a brief corps-a-corps)

Angelique
Take my horse. Then we're even.

Misere
 What?

(They push off. Misere lunges. As she does so, Angelique purposely drops her sword and opens her arms wide, taking Misere's point. She falls at C. This is a full-speed reprise of the slow-motion fight in silhouette that opened the play)

Misere *(kneeling beside Angelique, cradling her)*
 You little fool! What were you thinking?

Angelique
 I was thinking that I'd be "quality" for once. Was it believable?

Misere *(tearfully)*
 Bravo.

Angelique *(looking SL)*
 "But look, the morn…" *(dies)*

(Misere moves DC, picks up her cape, starts to lay it over Angelique. Maitre and the others move in)

Maitre
 Touching. Heart-rending. A death scene worthy of the immortals of the theatre.

Misere
 She **is** immortal. She **is** quality. None of you are either.

(She spins, whirling the cape into the Sergeant's face. As he struggles to clear it, she ducks under his arm, grabs his pistol hand, and squeezes his finger on the trigger. Pierre falls. Alphonse fires, but the bullet is taken by

the Sergeant. Misere lets him fall, dives for the sword she left on the ground. Alphonse has drawn his sword, cuts at her, misses as she rolls. She comes up with both her sword and Angelique's. Alphonse falls after a brief exchange at RC. Maitre draws his sword at RC and waits)

Maitre
Well, this wasn't in the script **I** wrote.

Misere
I'm just an amateur actress. Sometimes I forget my lines.

Maitre
And your place.

Misere
You have five thousand francs of mine.

Maitre *(patting his pocket)*
Right here. Come and collect it.

(They salute. Crossfade to DC spot. Misere walks into it, her cape draped over one arm)

Misere
Bonaparte went on to greater glory, before his inevitable decline. All stars fall, the scientists say. I wasn't there for the end. I buried poor Angelique in a German churchyard that night and took my leave of the Grand Armee. Went back to high-waisted dresses and all the feminine frippery I was expected to wear. Found a good man—there are some, believe it or not—who gave me a home and a daughter. Little Angie helps me run the bookshop. I bought it for exactly five thousand francs. *(tosses a gold coin in the air, catches it)* And I had one franc left over.

(She smiles, unfolds the cape, swirls it over her head. As it comes around in front, completely obscuring her, the lights black out)

0-595-27920-1

Printed in the United States
59442LVS00004B/192

9 780595 279203